I0820514

On Afghanistan's Plains

On Afghanistan's Plains

The Light Dragoons in Helmand 2006–2012

Allan Mallinson

Pen & Sword
MILITARY

First published in Great Britain in 2024 by
Pen & Sword Military
An imprint of Pen & Sword Books Limited
Yorkshire – Philadelphia

ISBN 978 1 03611 687 3

A CIP catalogue record for this book is
available from the British Library

Typeset by Mac Style
Printed in the UK by CPI Group (UK) Ltd, Croydon, CR0 4YY.

Pen & Sword Books Limited incorporates the imprints of After the Battle, Atlas, Archaeology, Aviation, Discovery, Family History, Fiction, History, Maritime, Military, Military Classics, Politics, Select, Transport, True Crime, Air World, Frontline Publishing, Leo Cooper, Remember When, Seaforth Publishing, The Praetorian Press, Wharncliffe Local History, Wharncliffe Transport, Wharncliffe True Crime and White Owl.

For a complete list of Pen & Sword titles please contact

PEN & SWORD BOOKS LIMITED
47 Church Street, Barnsley, South Yorkshire, S70 2AS, England
E-mail: enquiries@pen-and-sword.co.uk
Website: www.pen-and-sword.co.uk
or
PEN AND SWORD BOOKS
1950 Lawrence Road, Havertown, PA 19083, USA
E-mail: uspen-and-sword@casematepublishers.com
Website: www.penandswordbooks.com

When you're wounded and left on Afghanistan's plains,
And the women come out to cut up what remains,
Jest roll to your rifle and blow out your brains
An' go to your Gawd like a soldier.

"The Young British Soldier", Kipling.

"Western societies have learned how to kill on an enormous scale,
but they may still fight at a disadvantage against agrarian-age armies
who have not forgotten how to die, and know well enough how to kill."

Professor Sir Michael Howard OM CH CBE MC
How much can Technology change War? (2004)

"[W]hen I looked into their eyes, which were bloodshot with fatigue, I remember the extraordinary professionalism, competence and the sheer courage of those young men."

General Stanley McChrystal, Commander ISAF
Speech at The International Institute for Strategic Studies (2009)

Contents

Abbreviations

ADZ	Afghan Development Zone
AH	Attack Helicopter
ANA	Afghan National Army
ANP	Afghan National Police
ANSF	Afghan National Security Forces (ANA plus ANP)
APC	Armoured Personnel Carrier
ARRC	Allied Command Europe (Nato) Rapid Reaction Corps
BCR	Battle Casualty Replacement
BG	Battle Group
BRF	Brigade Reaction Force
CE	Combat Efficiency
CQMS	Company Quartermaster Sergeant
CSM	Company Sergeant Major
CVR(T)	Combat Vehicle, Reconnaissance (Tracked)
DAT	District Advisory Team
DROPS	Demountable Rack Offload and Pickup System
FOB	Forward Operating Base
FOO	Forward Observation Officer
FR	Force Reconnaissance
FSG	Fire Support Group
FUP	Forming-up Place
GPMG	General Purpose Machinegun
HE	High Explosive
IED	Improvized Explosive Device
ISAF	International Security Assistance Force
ISIS-K/ISKP	Islamic State of Iraq and Syria (Khorasan Province)

ISTAR	Intelligence, Surveillance, Target Acquisition, and Reconnaissance
JTAC	Joint Terminal Air Controller
MGB	Medium Girder Bridge
MOG	Manoeuvre Outreach Group
MRAP	Mine-Resistant Ambush Protected
MRX	Mission Rehearsal Exercise
NCO	Non-Commissioned Officer
NCOTT	NCO Training Team
OMLT	Operational Mentoring and Liaison Team
OP	Observation Post
PAT	Police Advisory Team
PMAG	Police mentoring and Advisory Group
PRT	Provincial Reconstruction Team
QRF	Quick reaction Force
RA	Royal Artillery
RAMC	Royal Army Medical Corps
RE	Royal Engineers
REME	Royal Electrical and Mechanical Engineers
RPG	Rocket-Propelled Grenade
SHQ	Squadron Headquarters
SNCO	Senior NCO
SSM	Squadron Sergeant Major
TACOM	Tactical Command
TACP	Tactical Air Control Party
TAOR	Tactical Area of Responsibility
TFH	Task Force Helmand
UOR	Urgent Operational Requirement
USMC	United States Marine Corps
VM	Vehicle Mechanic
VOR	Vehicle Off-Road

Introduction

"The best regiment in the army at present: consistently the best officered, the best recruited, and all round the most effective."

General Sir Charles (later Field Marshal Lord) Guthrie, Chief of the Defence Staff, 2001.

Since the formation of The Light Dragoons in 1992 by the amalgamation of the 13th/18th Royal Hussars (Queen Mary's Own) and 15th/19th The King's Royal Hussars, the regiment, or a part of it, has been continually – and at times it has seemed continuously – on operations. The peace that many thought would follow the end of the Cold War and the break-up of the Soviet Union, the mainspring of Communism (or at least of Marxism-Leninism), was to say the least illusory. In his 1992 book *The End of History and the Last Man*, the American writer Francis Fukuyama argued that humanity had now reached "not just … the passing of a particular period of post-war history, but the end of history as such: that is, the end-point of mankind's ideological evolution and the universalization of Western liberal democracy as the final form of human government." He didn't predict that war would actually cease, rather that what would happen in the future was that democracy would become more and more prevalent. The problem with this theory, of course, was that if universal democracy was "inevitable", existing democracies would be inclined to resort to war to hurry things along; and conversely, totalitarian regimes that believed it was *not* inevitable would fight with seemingly irrational tenacity – as the quote from Sir Michael Howard at the beginning of this book suggests.

Soon after the fall of the Soviet Union it was evident that in Europe the Cold War had kept a cap on nationalism, which now surfaced murderously in the Balkans. Consequently the regiment got to know Bosnia very well, and three Light Dragoons paid with their lives in what was meant to be a peacekeeping operation. Then the spectre of international terrorism, its aim no less than the destruction of Western liberal democracy itself, notably under the franchise of the ultra-extremist Islamist network al-Qaeda (the "base", or "foundation"), led the United States into war in Afghanistan and Iraq. As both a loyal bilateral ally and a Nato one too, Britain went to war alongside her. And so The Light Dragoons found themselves first in Basra and then in Helmand.

The four operational tours in Afghanistan between 2006 and 2012 are undoubtedly the most complex and dangerous that the regiment and its antecedents have experienced since the Second World War. But operational expertise isn't gained overnight. In a "family" regiment there is an ethos that is built up over generations. When asked why the Rifle Brigade had fought so well in the defence of Calais in 1940, their commanding officer replied simply, "The regiment had always fought well, and we were among friends." The ethos of The Light Dragoons, compounded of those of the two antecedent regiments, brilliantly blended in a model amalgamation, had been quickly proved in Bosnia, given a run-out in altogether different terrain in Iraq, and then tested beyond what few could have imagined in Afghanistan.

This book is intended to be a record of that achievement, a tribute to those who continued in and added to the ethos of The Light Dragoons, and a memorial to those who shed blood, especially those who did not come home.

Chapter One

History: We've Been Here Before

"Study history, study history,
in history lies all the secrets of Statecraft."

Churchill.

History is never short of quotes, but when it comes to Afghanistan, one in particular stands out as especially apt: "The past is never dead. It's not even past" (William Faulkner). For in Afghanistan, there's a lot of "past." There's even an Afghani joke about it, that a thousand years ago God visited the country and said as he left, "I can see what the problem is, but don't do anything till I come back."

Britain alone fought three wars there in less than a century – from 1839 to 1842, 1878 to 1880, and in 1919 – before the counter-insurgency campaign of 2002 to 2014 (and the continued support mission to 2021) in which The Light Dragoons played so prominent a part. A little of the background to the earlier wars might provide food for thought, not least in understanding, in Professor Howard's words, about "agrarian age armies who have not forgotten how to die, and know well enough how to kill."

The first Afghan war was pretty much a disaster for the British. In 1826, after a decade of civil war, Emir Dost Mohammad Barakzai (Dost Mohammad Khan) had come to the throne, but soon found himself caught between Great Britain and Russia, both of whom were manoeuvring for influence in the kingdom on the frontier of their expanding empires. What exactly the purpose was of what became known as the "Great Game" is in hindsight no clearer than it was at the time. The name was popularized by Rudyard Kipling in his novel *Kim* (1901) to describe the Anglo-Russian rivalry in Central Asia, and captured the sense of sport which permeated Victorian society, influenced by the reports of both officials and private adventurers enjoying the thrill of clandestine exploits beyond the frontiers of British India – reports that frequently embellished (or even invented) accounts of Russian intrigues and the fickle loyalties of tribal chiefs.

The British, believing that Dost Mohammad was either hostile to them or unable to resist Russian pressure, tried to intervene directly in Afghan affairs. First they negotiated, unsuccessfully, and then invaded, intending to restore the previous ruler to the throne. There was widespread rebellion, however, and in January 1842 they decided to quit Kabul. The retreat was very bloody indeed, on both sides, the British losing some 4,500 British and Indian troops, and 12,000 camp followers. And although in the summer British troops reoccupied Kabul, the following year the new governor-general of India decided on the evacuation of the entire country, and Dost Mohammad returned to the throne.

The game continued, but at lower intensity, until in 1878, with Russian influence growing, and with it the fear of meddling in India itself, a second invasion was launched. This Second Afghan War was carried out with considerably more efficiency than the first – it is too tempting not to wonder if this was because the 15th Hussars were part of the force that occupied Kandahar in January 1879 – and a treaty (Gandamak) was quickly concluded in which the new emir agreed to conduct his foreign affairs in accordance with "the wishes and advice" of the British government, and conceded the right for Britain to have a permanent representative in Kabul.

The triumph was as short-lived as the earlier one, however. The following year the British envoy and his escort were murdered. Troops were once again dispatched, under General Frederick Roberts VC – later Field Marshal Lord Roberts of Kandahar – and occupied Kabul. A new emir was found, a new boundary line with British India drawn, which was agreed by Russia, and things settled down, more or less. Except that the boundary, the Durand Line, named after the secretary of the British Indian government, was a time bomb. Twenty years later, "Young Winston" (Churchill) would earn his spurs in the province of Malakand on the North-West Frontier in a punitive confrontation astride the line.

Casualties in these later wars and expeditions weren't huge, but they were stinging, not least to pride, and cumulatively could lead to weariness or excesses. The Afghans proved recalcitrant neighbours in peace and elusive fighters in war, masters of ground and expert shots gifted with seemingly preternatural long sight. A hundred years before the term was used, Kipling wrote a poem about "asymmetric warfare", which summed up the character of war in Afghanistan, the "land of the Pashtuns", and which with considerable prescience he called *Arithmetic on the Frontier* (1886):

> A great and glorious thing it is
> To learn, for seven years or so,
> The Lord knows what of that and this,
> Ere reckoned fit to face the foe —
> The flying bullet down the Pass,
> That whistles clear: 'All flesh is grass.'
>
> Three hundred pounds per annum spent
> On making brain and body meeter
> For all the murderous intent
> Comprised in 'villanous saltpetre!'
> And after — ask the Yusufzaies
> What comes of all our 'ologies.
>
> A scrimmage in a Border Station —
> A canter down some dark defile —
> Two thousand pounds of education

Drops to a ten-rupee jezail —
The Crammer's boast, the Squadron's pride,
Shot like a rabbit in a ride!

No proposition Euclid wrote,
No formulae the text-books know,
Will turn the bullet from your coat,
Or ward the tulwar's downward blow.
Strike hard who cares — shoot straight who can —
The odds are on the cheaper man.

One sword-knot stolen from the camp
Will pay for all the school expenses
Of any Kurrum Valley scamp
Who knows no word of moods and tenses,
But, being blessed with perfect sight,
Picks off our messmates left and right.

With home-bred hordes the hillsides teem,
The troop-ships bring us one by one,
At vast expense of time and steam,
To slay Afridis where they run.
The 'captives of our bow and spear'
Are cheap — alas! as we are dear.

Later, in *The Courting of Dinah Shadd*, Kipling has Private Ortheris lamenting:

I fired a shot at a Afghan,
The beggar 'e fired again,
An' I lay on my bed with a 'ole in my 'ed,
An' missed the next campaign!

Afghan tribesmen certainly sharpened the British army's fighting skills. But the savagery of these wars became particularly marked. Kipling again:

> When you're wounded and left on Afghanistan's plains,
> And the women come out to cut up what remains,
> Jest roll to your rifle and blow out your brains
> An' go to your Gawd like a soldier.

When in 1914 Ottoman Turkey entered the war on the side of the Central Powers (Germany and Austria-Hungary), Constantinople did its best to incite *jihad*, that is, to make it a fight against the enemies of Islam, in particular with the British in India, on whose native army much of the Empire now depended. Naturally, in Afghanistan there was widespread support for Turkey, but Habibullah Khan, emir since 1901, modernising and pro-British, managed to maintain a policy of non-involvement, which allowed Delhi to send a good many troops (including the 13th Hussars) to the Middle East who would otherwise have been tied down in observation or worse on the North-West Frontier. However, Habibullah paid the price in 1919, assassinated by anti-British supporters of his son Amanullah Khan, who promptly took possession of the throne and declared total independence from Great Britain. This declaration launched the Third Anglo-Afghan War.

It was a short and relatively bloodless one, though, a series of skirmishes between an ineffective Afghan army and a British Indian army not yet recovered from the Great War. In August a peace treaty recognizing the absolute independence of Afghanistan was concluded. Ominously, however, even before the ink was dry the Afghans signed a treaty of friendship with the Bolshevik regime in Moscow, one of the first states to recognize the new Soviet government. A "special relationship" thence evolved which ultimately helped no one. In 1973, the Socialist prime minister Daoud Khan instigated a coup that overthrew the monarchy and made him president. Five years later the Communist People's Democratic Party of Afghanistan deposed him, but anti-communist Islamic guerrillas, commonly called *mujahideen* ("those who make jihad"), backed by the CIA, at once began a civil war against the Kabul government. Among these guerrillas was a Saudi Arabian – the seventeenth child (allegedly of more than fifty) of a billionaire construction magnate – called Osama bin Laden, leader – "First General Emir" – of al-Qaeda. The following year, 1979, the Soviet Union invaded Afghanistan in support of the communist government.

It was arguably the Soviet regime's worst misjudgement of the Cold War (which is saying something). It soon became the proverbial quagmire: the Soviet army suffered 15,000 dead and countless wounded until in 1988 the United States, Pakistan, Afghanistan and Moscow signed an agreement by which Soviet troops would withdraw and Afghanistan would return to non-aligned status. In 1992, in the wake of the collapse of the Soviet Union, various rebel groups together with newly rebellious government troops, overthrew the communist President Najibullah. For a while it looked like another episode in "the end of history" and the glide into universal liberal democracy, which liberals generally took to be a cue to rest on their arms, and some conservatives – "neocons" (neo-conservatives) – took as an invitation to hasten the glide with military interventions. History, however, was not dead yet. The transitional government proclaimed an Islamic republic, but the mujahideen proved to be fragmental and soon Kabul was a city under siege and the countryside outside the capital slipped into chaos as the various factions warred amongst themselves and with what passed for government forces. The strongest proved to be the Taliban ("students"), a particularly puritanical Islamist group led by Mullah Mohammad Omar, which augmented by volunteers from various foreign Islamist groups sheltering in Afghanistan had by the middle of 1996 seized control of most of the country and occupied Kabul. Just a small part of northern Afghanistan remained in the hands of a loose coalition of less militant mujahideen forces known as the Northern Alliance. Fighting continued in a stalemate for the next five years until the world-changing events of 9/11.

The exact moments at which the two hijacked planes crashed into the "Twin Towers" on 11 September 2001 are now erased from the mainstream media. Taste and decency demand it, and also reason: repetition risks dulling the senses. Yet although the choice of weapon and target far exceeded the evil of the Japanese surprise attack on Pearl Harbor (a day that in President Franklin Roosevelt's words would "live in infamy"), the attacks on the World Trade Center and the Pentagon, and the heroically thwarted attack on the White House, shared with Pearl Harbor the shock of sudden vulnerability – and in consequence provoked the same seismic shift of US strategy. Writing of the opening battle of the English Civil War, Edgehill some 350 years earlier, Kipling concluded:

> The first dry rattle of new-drawn steel
> Changes the world today!

Had he been alive on 9/11 he might have been moved to write that the twisted skeleton of blackened steel changes the world today.[1]

Forty-eight hours after the attacks a defiant President George W. Bush stood amid the rubble at "Ground Zero" (significantly, the term used of the point on the earth's surface directly above or below a nuclear explosion), his hand on the shoulder of one of the New York firemen who had borne the brunt of the heroic rescue effort, and spoke to the crowd through a megaphone. When a distant voice called out, "George, we can't hear you!" Bush smiled and answered: "I can hear

1. Though this, that it was an existential game-changer for the US (and therefore the world), was not universally acknowledged at the time – a dangerous disconnect between British and American strategic thinking which continued up to the final withdrawal from Afghanistan in 2021.

you! I can hear you, the rest of the world can hear you, and the people who knocked these buildings down will hear all of us soon!"

A week later, addressing Congress, Bush expanded on his extemporary remark:

> Americans are asking, "How will we fight and win this war?" We will direct every resource at our command – every means of diplomacy, every tool of intelligence, every instrument of law enforcement, every financial influence, and every necessary weapon of war – to the destruction and to the defeat of the global terror network. Now, this war will not be like the war against Iraq a decade ago, with a decisive liberation of territory and a swift conclusion. It will not look like the air war above Kosovo two years ago, where no ground troops were used and not a single American was lost in combat. Our response involves far more than instant retaliation and isolated strikes. Americans should not expect one battle, but a lengthy campaign unlike any other we have ever seen. It may include dramatic strikes visible on TV and covert operations secret even in success. We will starve terrorists of funding, turn them one against another, drive them from place to place until there is no refuge or no rest …

Sitting close by the president in Congress was Tony Blair, Britain's prime minister, who had flown to Washington in a show of solidarity and to offer support (though critically he had not taken with him the chief of the defence staff). Bush spoke of several countries which had shown their support, then added: "America has no truer friend than Great Britain. Once again, we are joined together in a great cause. I'm so honoured the British prime minister has crossed an ocean to show his unity with America. Thank you for coming, friend."

Going to Washington was, of course, what Churchill had done in the aftermath of Pearl Harbor. Blair's ocean crossing would likewise define the British military response, though he played his hand with less acumen than Churchill did in the Second World War. Unlike Churchill, Blair could never be criticized for taking a close interest in military detail.

Within a month of the attacks the United States had begun its counter-offensive, the "War on Terror." Afghanistan had been a haven and training ground for al-Qaeda, which had carried out the 9/11 attacks as well as bombings and assassinations over the previous decade in East Africa, the Middle East and western Asia, and the Taliban had refused US demands to extradite Osama bin Laden, who had again taken refuge in the country after his expulsion from Sudan in 1996.

The US campaign to oust the Taliban (Operation Enduring Freedom) was mounted under Article 5 of the North Atlantic Charter[2] and enjoyed widespread if not always vocal international support. It was a brilliantly conceived and well-executed application of high-tech intelligence, Special Forces (including British), air power (including the RAF)[3], and the armies of the various anti-Taliban warlords known officially as the United Islamic Front for the Salvation of Afghanistan, and commonly as the Northern Alliance.

By the middle of November, Kabul was in the hands of the Americans and their allies, and by the end of December it looked as if all that was left was merely mopping up. Indeed the historian and commentator Sir John Keegan, writing in the *Daily Telegraph*, compared the apparent

2. Article 5 of the North Atlantic Charter states that 'an armed attack against one or more of [the allies] in Europe or North America shall be considered an attack against them all and ... [each] will assist the Party or Parties so attacked by taking forthwith, individually and in concert with the other Parties, such action as it deems necessary, including the use of armed force, to restore and maintain the security of the North Atlantic area.'
3. The initial attacks saw the first use of the Royal Navy's Tomahawk Land Attack ["Cruise"] Missile (TLAM). They all missed the target by 400 metres to the northeast, the programmers having failed to take into account the earth's rotation when inputting the flight path. A salutary, and expensive, lesson in the limitations of stand-off warfare.

victory with one of the great turning points in the military history of the British Empire: "The collapse of Taliban resistance in northern Afghanistan and the fall of Kabul may stand as one of the most remarkable reversals of military fortune since Kitchener's victory at Omdurman in the Sudan in 1898."

But despite the ferocious battles in the mountains of south-east Afghanistan, in which lay the cave complex of Tora Bora to which many Taliban had bolted, the key al-Qaeda leaders could not be found. Those Taliban who had not been killed in last stands at Tora Bora fled across the border into Pakistan.

US and British forces and their Afghan allies now began to consolidate. A *loya jirga* (grand council) of tribal leaders and former exiles, in effect an interim Afghan government, was established in Kabul under the sophisticated tribal leader Hamid Karzai, and a Nato-led International Security Assistance Force (ISAF) mandated by the UN Security Council to secure Kabul and surrounding areas from attack by the Taliban, al-Qaeda and factional warlords. At the same time, military attention also turned to civil projects to win over the hearts and minds of those Afghans further afield who were indifferent to who ruled in Kabul.

The Taliban had not given up, however, and both American and British troops were in action throughout 2002, although far enough from Kabul as to reinforce the general impression that peace prevailed, and democratic and economic progress was being made. British efforts were in the main concentrated on "provincial reconstruction", in which the army (with around 1,500 troops) was – in broad terms – meant to provide conditions of security within which the civilian agencies could operate. However, both London and Washington increasingly took their military eyes off the ball, while the civil agencies seemed unable or unwilling to play the game at all. The experienced British major-general in charge of the multinational "security assistance force", John McColl, was replaced by a newly promoted colonel to head the British contingent – Simon Levey, who had just relinquished command of The Light Dragoons.[4] His task was to "reduce the footprint" from about 2,000. When it got to just 300 he was told that that would do.

It all looked like the early symptoms of "mission-accomplished" syndrome. The initial strategic objective, to eject al-Qaeda from Afghanistan had been rapidly achieved – *too* easily and too quickly perhaps to satisfy US demands for revenge post 9/11. And this in turn prompted advanced thinkers in Washington, "neocons", to think ambitiously about nation-building in the West's image; and so "mission accomplished" turned into "mission creep." And, some might say, in defiance of history.[5]

It was a cruel illusion (or delusion). President Karzai's new government began increasingly to struggle in their attempts to secure centralized authority over the country against a surprisingly powerful Taliban pushback – a full-blown insurgency indeed. And the military began

4. So impressed with McColl was Karzai that the by then President (a republic having been established in 2004 after three years' transitional government) is reputed to have made enticing offers for him to pay back the Queen's shilling and take his instead. Blair later made McColl his special envoy to Afghanistan, and when Karzai turned down the former leader of the Liberal-Democrats, Paddy Ashdown, as the UN nominee as high representative in Kabul, he asked again for McColl (by then Deputy Supreme Allied [Nato] Commander Europe) instead. Here were shades of the North-West Frontier and the "Great Game."
5. Neoconservatism is (or, at least, was) a political movement with its origins in the US during the 1960s among liberal "hawks" who had become disenchanted with the increasingly pacifist foreign policy of the Democratic Party, as well as being appalled by the left-wing counter-culture, in particular the Vietnam protests. Neocons advocated the promotion of democracy and interventionism in international affairs, gaining encouragement from the collapse of the Soviet Union in 1992, which they saw (and who could blame them?) as a victory for President Ronald Reagan's uncompromising stand against communism. Seeing the future, then, as a constant glide into liberal democracy, they sought to speed that glide wherever they could. UK MoD was sceptical, but there was beguiling encouragement from other agencies – including intelligence and development – who saw it also as an opportunity to gain more funds, with the justification that "90% of the heroin on the streets of UK comes from Afghanistan." And there was many a senior officer who saw it as (a) an exit strategy for Iraq, and (b) an opportunity to regain fighting reputation after the debacles of Basra.

increasingly to struggle in their attempts to form Clausewitz's "first, the supreme, the most far-reaching act of judgement": to establish the kind of war on which they were embarking.

It was no place for a "light footprint."

Chapter Two

Operation Herrick: What Kind of War? And What's in a Name?

"Herrick" was the codename by which Britain's operations in Afghanistan were conducted from 2002.[1] Codenames are randomly generated and chosen as appropriate (in theory at least) by the Ministry of Defence. "Telic", the codename under which the regiment deployed twice to Iraq, is an adjective meaning (of an action) "directed or tending to a definite end or goal." It must have seemed apt at the time of choosing. "Herrick" is a family name (Robert Herrick was the 17th Century poet famous for "Gather ye rosebuds while ye may") thought to originate in the Norse/Germanic *heer riks:* literally "army ruler", or more colloquially, "warlord." If this was known at the time of choosing, it must have seemed particularly apt too. The British army was about to become one of many warlords in Afghanistan.

Operation Herrick began inoffensively enough, however. At first its primary component remained the 300 or so troops providing security in Kabul and helping to train the new Afghan National Army (ANA), but the following year the numbers more than doubled when several "provincial reconstruction teams" (PRTs) and a rapid reaction force were established in north-western Afghanistan. Meanwhile, the number of troops based in Kabul was also rising – to 1,300 – and with

1. First was Veritas (Latin: "Truth") consisting of support during the US invasion in October 2001. Second was Fingal (a legendary Irish/Scots giant and eponymous cave dweller: from the Irish – and equally apt – *Fine Gall*: "foreign tribe"), involving leadership and a 2,000-strong contribution for a newly formed ISAF in Kabul after December 2001. Several months later, command was transferred to Turkey (a NATO member), and the British contingent scaled back to 300.

an RAF detachment of six fighters at Kandahar airfield in support of the Americans.

Then early in 2006, some 70 states and fifteen international organizations – not least Nato – took part in a conference in London chaired by the British prime minister Tony Blair, President Karzai and UN Secretary General Kofi Annan to agree a concept of international cooperation. The conference concluded with the promulgation of the "The Afghanistan Compact", in which all the participants,

> "Determined to strengthen their partnership to improve the lives of Afghan people, and to contribute to national, regional, and global peace and security;
>
> Affirming their shared commitment to continue… to work toward a stable and prosperous Afghanistan, with good governance and human rights protection for all under the rule of law, and to maintain and strengthen that commitment over the term of this Compact and beyond;
>
> Recognising the courage and determination of Afghans who, by defying violent extremism and hardship, have laid the foundations for a democratic, peaceful, pluralistic and prosperous state based on the principles of Islam;
>
> Noting the full implementation of the Bonn Agreement [the initial series of agreements in December 2001 following the US invasion to re-create the State of Afghanistan]…;
>
> Mindful that Afghanistan's transition to peace and stability is not yet assured, and that strong international engagement will continue to be required to address remaining challenges;
>
> Resolved to overcome the legacy of conflict in Afghanistan by setting conditions for sustainable economic growth and development; strengthening state institutions and civil society; removing remaining terrorist threats; meeting the challenge of

> counter-narcotics; rebuilding capacity and infrastructure; reducing poverty; and meeting basic human needs;
>
> Have agreed to this Afghanistan Compact."

As far as the various national military contingents in Afghanistan were concerned, however, the most significant specification – though its significance was not recognized and acted on initially with anything like the address that was needed – was that "a professional and ethnically balanced Afghan National Army with up to 70,000 soldiers is to be established and fully functional by 2010" while "The police being formed is to provide reliable security in the country and at the borders."

ISAF now moved up several gears to take over progressively more responsibility from the discrete but inevitably overlapping US Operation Enduring Freedom (the name extended beyond the initial intervention in 2001). It became a four-star command, and in May 2006 the multinational (NATO) HQ Allied Rapid Reaction Corps (ARRC) deployed from its base in Gloucestershire as the force headquarters for nine months, the first time a standing rather than an ad hoc headquarters would be in charge. In command was the British General Sir David Richards, with a mandate to align the campaign with the "Afghanistan Compact", not least through his membership of the Afghan Presidential Advisory Group.[2]

---

2. During the ARRC's nine-month stint, ISAF's area of operations doubled in size, encompassing the whole country, troop numbers growing from 9,500 to more than 35,000 as a result. Richards, a keen student of the British army's successful counter-insurgency campaign in Malaya (1948–60), put considerable effort into blending the different threads of the counter-Taliban campaign – political, military, security, humanitarian and developmental – at local, regional and national levels – and sometimes at international level, not least because with the expansion of ISAF's area of operations, for the first time there was a common border with Pakistan. It was not so much like turning a supertanker as boarding a smaller one, setting a new course, then refitting and enlarging it while still at sea. But the nine months probably rescued ISAF from early defeat.

Meanwhile there was to be a major shift of emphasis for the British. Responsibility for the PRTs in the north-west was handed over to other national contingents to allow them to refocus on south Afghanistan. The defence secretary, John Reid, announced that Britain would send a PRT with several thousand extra troops to Helmand province for at least three years as part of the gradual expansion of ISAF's area of responsibility from Kabul to the rest of the country in various "Afghan Development Zones" (ADZ). Reid planned an initial strength of 5,700 in all, stabilizing at about 4,500 for the rest of the deployment on six-month rotation as before. Announcing the increase, he was at pains to explain that the 3,500 (a brigade's worth) extra troops were being deployed to help the reconstruction effort, but he added not unreasonably that

> "Although our mission to Afghanistan is primarily reconstruction, it is a complex and dangerous mission because the terrorists will want to destroy the economy and the legitimate trade and the government that we are helping to build up. Of course, our mission is not counter-terrorism but one of the tasks that we may have to accomplish in order to achieve our strategic mission will be to defend our own troops and the people we are here to defend and to pre-empt, on occasion, terrorist attacks on us. If this didn't involve the necessity to use force we wouldn't send soldiers."

He distanced the operation from that of the Americans (Enduring Freedom), saying it was "fundamentally different to that of the US forces elsewhere in Afghanistan … We are in the south to help and protect the Afghan people construct their own democracy." But then, in a sort of throwaway line which would encapsulate a decade's woolliness in Westminster's military thinking, and having already implied that there was no unity of effort in the country, he added: "We would be perfectly happy to leave in three years and without firing one shot because our job is to protect the reconstruction."

While such hopes of peace were wholly worthy they would soon reveal a dangerous misappreciation of the situation in Afghanistan, and in Helmand province in particular, as well as quite remarkable hubris. For the Taliban at once declared they would oppose the efforts. Within months of Reid's announcement forty servicemen had been killed, half of them in Helmand in one month alone, for 16 Air Assault Brigade, which was to be the basis of the reinforcement ("Herrick 4" – the fourth six-monthly deployment of troops), at once began trying to pre-empt the attacks, as Reid had intimated, as well as fighting them off. The brigade commander, Brigadier Ed Butler, a former SAS commanding officer, seemed determined to take the fight to the Taliban rather than await the inevitable – as he saw it – counter-offensive, though in fact in terms of available combat power he had not much more than an augmented parachute battalion.

In the late summer and autumn there were daily and heavy fire-fights with the Taliban, and platoon-size (thirty men) standing patrols dotted about Helmand in defended houses had to resort increasingly to calling in fire from artillery, RAF (and allied) ground-attack aircraft and the Apache attack-helicopter (AH). It was, said the defenders, with the grim humour honed over two centuries of colonial fighting, "Rorke's Drift every day". Strategically, Brigadier Butler appeared to be content, though, for he believed they were "bringing on the Taliban early", and would thereby have them at a disadvantage. In many ways this accorded with the received wisdom of communist-revolutionary warfare – although of course the Taliban were anything but communist – that the enemy should be worn down by ambush and sabotage while building up conventional strength to take on and defeat the conventionally-organized enemy in open battle. It had been a notably successful feature of Mao's campaign against the nationalist forces in China, and also that of Ho Chi Minh in French Indo-China. If the Taliban were trying to follow this blueprint they appeared to have dangerously accelerated the process in hurling their fighters against a preponderance of conventional firepower. Brigadier

Butler claimed tactical success, but it would be short lived. Besides, while huge amounts of ordnance killed Taliban in large numbers, the collateral damage was also heavy, and what little progress there was in "nation-building" – the whole object of Reid's announcement – was soon either put on hold or even reversed.

There were criticisms of the way Brigadier Butler spread his forces in "penny packets" around Helmand – and indeed the Chief of the General Staff, Sir Richard Dannatt, although he had no direct operational authority, "advised" a redeployment in face of the mounting casualties – but Brigadier Butler himself appeared to feel he'd been given no choice in the absence of strategic clarity. In his post-operational report he wrote of "the lack of early, formal political direction and a strictly enforced manning cap [upper limit of troop numbers], established upon apparently best case rather than most likely or worst case planning assumptions and taking little account of the enemy vote". He also complained that getting the right equipment and in the right numbers was hampered because the MoD and Treasury were unwilling to commit funds to Urgent Operational [equipment] Requirements (UOR) prior to any formal political announcements. But he put his finger on the real essence of the problem when he spoke of "unrealistic timescale that foresaw no offensive operations", for Clausewitz's *first* rule – "to enter the field with an army as strong as possible" – was thereby ignored. Clausewitz added ruefully that "This [rule] sounds very like a common place, but still is really not so." Indeed it is not. Brigadier Butler resigned eighteen months after returning from Afghanistan, as did the commanding officer of the Parachute battalion, who had also been dismayed at the inadequate treatment of his wounded soldiers on evacuation to Britain.

The preoccupation of British troops in Helmand that first summer had been "kinetic" – fighting the Taliban. To a large extent this was inevitable. Until the Afghans were themselves able to provide security for the people of Helmand, the British (and their allied contingents) would have to do so. A forward presence was therefore necessary. But as the Taliban opposed that presence as an "article of faith", as well as seeing the province as a key proving ground for their ability to take and hold territory from Nato-led Afghan National Security Forces (ANSF – the ANA and police), the fighting would grow in intensity, to the detriment of training the ANA. Indeed, the more the Taliban could distract ISAF, the longer it would take to make the ANA capable of taking responsibility for security.

In the later nineteenth century British army officers began developing subtle humint and low-tech skills, mastering tribal languages and acquiring considerable ethnographic techniques – in India especially, sometimes on secondment to the Indian Political Service as district administrators or as advisors to the princely states independent of the British Raj, and of course became players in the Great Game. Understanding and respecting the ways of native peoples – speaking their language literally and metaphorically – became a point of pride, the politically nuanced officer thereby able to punch above his weight in dealing with feudal rulers, confident of the real weight that backed it. The concept entered the collective mind of the army. On withdrawal from empire it largely left that mind, however, except to a degree in Special Forces.

Thus the British army had embarked on a mission of subtlety in Helmand, but not initially with the tools for the job, or even an agreed understanding of what was the job or the tools. That autumn, they started to reach "cessation of hostilities" agreements with local Taliban forces around the district centres that they'd held in the summer. Under the terms of the agreements, both sides were meant to withdraw from the conflict zone. It was tacit acceptance that troop numbers were just too low to hold the key bases in Helmand requested by President Karzai. It was also a setback for the Taliban, who'd been desperate to consolidate their gains but had been losing men in troubling numbers. They would have to play a longer game, and they believed they could, that time was on their side. They coined a slogan indeed: "You may have the watches, but we have the time."

This was clever, because it played on what the Taliban knew would be the weakness of the international community: strategic patience. The US was still haunted by the long war in Vietnam, and severely pressed by the insurgency in Iraq following the 2003 invasion, which the British were eager to quit too.[3] So the Taliban began to adapt their tactics. Instead of hurling themselves at strongly defended positions, they considered the "arithmetic on the frontier". The term "asymmetric warfare" describes conflict between conventionally equipped, high-tech regulars and an enemy who takes them on, deliberately or through no choice, at a lower level of military technology. The boy David's sling against the chink in the giant Goliath's armour isn't a bad analogy. The low-tech force relies on patience and pin-prick attacks, often the IED, the improvized explosive device (which in the terrain of Helmand could be huge), aiming at the exhaustion of the opponent's political will to continue the fight in the face of steady – if comparatively quite small – losses. The conventional force must either bring the other to battle "in the open" – tempting them to believe that "one big push" will finish the job, and that they have the strength to do so – or else adapt the enemy's own tactics to fight at the low-tech level even better than he does. The latter requires a great deal of "humint" especially (human intelligence, as opposed to that gathered by technical means), as the enemy's methods of communicating and operating will likely not be easily susceptible to non-human penetration. Humint was at a premium as far as ISAF and the ANSF were concerned. One Light Dragoons officer (Major John Godfrey), writing of this more asymmetrical phase, gave the Taliban handsome praise: "The average Taliban fighter is sly, fearless and a master of camouflage and concealment. He is not stupid and understands our rules of engagement as well as we do. Unless he will

3. British troops in quasi-divisional strength had assisted the US in the invasion of Iraq in 2003, which Washington viewed as part of its "war on terror" – as well as unfinished business from the First Gulf War (1991) – and found themselves seriously on the back foot in Basra when they underestimated the scale and nature of the post-invasion insurgency.

lose face or ground that he wishes to retain, he will simply blend into the local population and observe you. If he spots a perceived weakness, however, he will react. The trick then is to convince him that you are weak enough for him to take you on; not that easy to do as nobody wants to initiate a well-prepared ambush on ground of the enemy's choosing, and if you suspect that he is there, the natural reaction is to look for him in strength. Contacts were most frequently therefore initiated at extremely close range and in extremely close country." And movement made constantly tense by the IED threat.

Fighting continued throughout the winter of 2006–7, British and allied troops – including Special Forces – increasingly pro-active. It was in this operational context that The Light Dragoons had their first taste of Afghanistan – on Herrick 5, when in October 2006, 3rd Commando Brigade, Royal Marines, some 4,500 servicemen and servicewomen – relieved 16th Air Assault Brigade.

Chapter Three

Herrick 5: October 2006–April 2007

The Legion[1]

The 3rd Commando Brigade hoped to consolidate their positions in the various towns across the province, reducing their presence where possible in exchange for adopting a more mobile approach. There was also considerable pressure to make progress on the reconstruction effort. Despite at times the brutal winter conditions, the Taliban maintained their presence and, like the Paras before them, the men of 3 Commando Brigade soon became engaged in some of the heaviest fighting of modern times. The main combat power was provided by 42 Commando, 45 Commando taking on the ANA mentoring role, with 29 Commando Regiment Royal Artillery, 59 Independent Commando Squadron Royal Engineers, 28 Engineer Regiment, and the Commando Logistics Regiment in support – and C Squadron, Light Dragoons.

C Squadron ("The Legion"), under command of Major Ben Warrack, a veteran of Iraq (and not long back from there, with the rest of the squadron – just five months between leaving Basra and beginning pre-Herrick training) as well as of Northern Ireland and two tours of the Balkans, provided the formation recce squadron (FR) – ie the

---

1. On formation of The Light Dragoons, the new C Squadron continued the use of the nickname "The Legion", acquired at the time of the 1922 amalgamation of the 15th and the 19th Hussars. The 19th Hussars, having initially been disbanded and then rapidly re-raised for – in the words of the new CIGS who reversed the disbandment policy – "amalgamation rather than oblivion", had formed C Squadron of the new 15th/19th Hussars, and hence taken the name in ironic reference to the Foreign Legion.

Helmand task force's. 3 Commando Brigade had the advantage of coming forewarned and prepared for a fight, whereas the air assault brigade had been caught somewhat on the hop in the transition from provincial reconstruction to countering a violent insurgency. They also had a better "force package" than the air assault brigade, able to put more troops on the ground, and a complete regiment of sappers to focus on reconstruction and development.

The squadron deployed to Camp Bastion in mid-October and by the end of the month were ready for tasking, having rapidly applied bar-armour (which looked like close-slatted fencing) to the Scimitars and supporting CVR(T)s, and deployed on a two-day shake-out patrol in the desert. Training had been in the expectation of high-intensity fighting. Once in theatre, however, it became immediately clear that the six months would be different from that of the previous squadron (D Squadron, Household Cavalry Regiment – HCR). They were to remain as an intact force in the ISTAR (intelligence, surveillance, target acquisition and reconnaissance) role rather than being split up and sent to the various platoon houses, and manoeuvre as a whole in the desert in the southern area of Helmand, uncharted territory. Their mission was to find, interdict and disrupt enemy forces in the south, tailor-made for both their "DNA" as a recce squadron, and their vehicles.

The squadron, made up of three scimitar troops and one support troop with squadron headquarters (SHQ), fitters of the Royal Electrical and Mechanical Engineers (REME), and the ambulance, would provide much-needed heft to the specialist brigade patrols troop and together made up the Brigade Reconnaissance Force (BRF). As well as their traditional recce role The Light Dragoons would also prove invaluable in support of set-piece deliberate operations by 42 Commando, bringing crew-served, under-armour weapon-systems to the fight day and night. Next-generation thermal imagery would prove to be a game-changer on many a highly kinetic occasion.

Operations were to be based on what was known as a "Manoeuvre Outreach Group" (MOG – and hence, inevitably, the concept was known as "mogging"), in essence a battalion-group sitting in the middle of the desert in Garmsir (or Garm Ser) district able to flex various force elements to "bespoke" operations. These, naturally, were focussed on the Helmand River valley – the "Green Zone" – or rather some 60 miles of it, 3–6 miles wide, in mid-Helmand. Outside the zone the terrain was sparsely populated, flat or at most slightly undulating, and dusty, although astride the river the zone was a more complex topography – deep canals, irrigation ditches and compounds. Garmsir "town" itself was a rubble-strewn place whose population had grown, and was growing, simply because it was the only crossing point of the Helmand for miles.

The squadron therefore found itself conducting a wide range of operations: "soft effects" such as reassurance patrols, identifying future projects to help develop the local community, and intelligence gathering. But there were, of course, "kinetic exchanges" – fire-fights.

The first major encounter with the Taliban took place in mid-November when the squadron attempted to prove a river crossing (find a place they could cross without bridging). Throughout the Green Zone the problem was not just in crossing the Helmand itself but the multitude of canals and irrigation ditches on the approaches and beyond. The squadron approached the west bank relatively easily, and went firm. Squadron Sergeant-Major (SSM) Howard ("Chuck") Berry manned the crossing point with 3rd Troop acting as close bank protection while 1st and 2nd Troops crossed the river to find a route through the maze of ditches and canals. On pushing further south it became apparent that there was no way through; and then came a noticeable shift in "atmospherics." The general pattern of life seemed to change, with work in the fields stopping, groups of young men gathering, and women and children disappearing.

The Taliban opened fire on three sides and made to get behind the two troops to cut them off. 1st Troop, slowed by a mechanical problem, managed to get back to the crossing point, but the Taliban – estimates of fifty or so, with heavy machineguns and rocket-propelled grenades (RPGs) – succeeded in cutting off the withdrawal of 2nd Troop by a combination of accurate mortar fire and slick flanking techniques. The troop leader, Lieutenant James Townsend-Rose, his Scimitar's engine on fire, the fan belt having broken (the extra armour added some two tons to the Scimitar's usual eight), decided to take a gamble and try to cross the river at an unproven point. In doing so he fully submerged his driver, Trooper Joe Cooperwaite, whose day sight had been damaged by a machinegun round moments earlier and so had had to open up the hatch. The gamble paid off, but the contact had lasted for nearly 2 hours, the squadron firing over 400 rounds of 30mm main armament and 6,000 rounds of GPMG (general purpose machinegun).[2]

"We own the desert, but the Taliban own the green areas," Major Warrack told the Daily Telegraph's defence correspondent, Tom Coghlan, who spent a fortnight with the squadron. As Coghlan wrote in a report for the Telegraph, "While the Dragoons can appear without warning in the desert, the green areas negate many of their advantages. The vegetation provides cover for the Taliban while narrow tracks and concentrations of walled houses slow the Scimitars and funnel them into potential ambush sites."

The second major encounter occurred on 5 December. Z Company, 45 Commando, had planned an operation to probe south of Garmsir, with the squadron providing flank protection and fire support: 3rd Troop in intimate support, 1st Troop flanking fire support, 4th Troop in reserve. 1st Troop moved into position on the western bank of the river just as dawn was breaking and immediately spotted eight Taliban. 3rd Troop moved across the bridge and took up positions among the three troops (platoons) of Z Company. Shortly afterwards, H-Hour was signalled by a salvo of 51mm HE (high explosive) mortar fire from 4th Troop and the SSM. This allowed the marines to start their advance, slowly and deliberately, clearing compounds and trenches as

2. Trooper Cooperwaite's father, Staff-Sergeant Bob Cooperwaite, was SSM A Squadron in Swanton Morley. Indeed, so legend has it, on Herricks 5 and 6 the regiment deployed with six father and son combinations. The Cooperwaites subsequently served together on Herrick 10.

they went. 3rd Troop cut about to put direct fire onto many of these positions, the night sights picking up heat signatures of Taliban in the long grass, invisible to the naked eye. The squadron summary report spoke of the "accuracy and firepower of the 30mm being proved time and again, destroying compound walls, obliterating enemy fire trenches from 2km and taking on individual targets at 1500m."

The operation was going well, the Taliban withdrawing, their fire inaccurate and their tactics crude. About midday, however, the atmosphere changed; the enemy had appeared to recover, the fire becoming heavier and more accurate, the tactics coordinated and effective. Air assets were now called in, including Apache AH, Harrier ground-attack aircraft and US fighter-bombers, and the light guns of 7 (Sphinx) Battery, 29 Regiment, fired over 150 rounds of HE. In the early afternoon two marines were hit by cannon fire from a US close-support aircraft on its strafing run. The squadron Samaritan (CVR(T) ambulance), escorted by 4th Troop, extracted the casualties to squadron HQ where the medics treated them before evacuation by helicopter, although one of the marines died subsequently.

The withdrawal started later in the afternoon as planned, the squadron covering the company's disengagement by increasing fire to dissuade the Taliban from following-up, the marines managing to break contact without further loss at 4.30pm after an intense ten hours' fighting. Coghlan described it vividly:

> The hardest day of their tour came on the 5th December when the Dragoons took part in one of five separate full-scale attacks so far mounted against Taliban bases south of the town of Garmsir. Despite the operations, the insurgents have clung to well dug in systems of trenches and deep tunnels which have proved impervious even to airstrikes by American B1 heavy bombers.
>
> The Dragoons had to fight their way into the town to aid a dozen Royal Marines fighting around 200 Taliban fighters.

The troops blasted through compound walls using explosive charges while under Taliban fire. Sergeant Simpson a Royal Engineer attached to the Dragoons [who subsequently transferred to the regiment, was commissioned and became the Quartermaster] used 40 charges and was twice concussed by the blast from his own explosives. Another Dragoon, Sergeant Mick Wilkinson, was trapped outside his vehicle by heavy fire and reduced to shooting back at the Taliban fighters around him with his pistol.

A Scimitar that reached the trapped Marines reversed back again a mile and a half firing back at the Taliban with the Marines running alongside.

"When we got back there was huge adrenaline," said Captain Will Jelf, 28, the Dragoon squadron second in command. "We were exhausted. Some people were physically sick."

Several of the younger men in the unit have suffered the after-effects of such extreme situations.

"You can't measure courage until you are facing danger," said Warrant Officer 2nd Class Dale McKenzie, the Squadron sergeant major. "Some of the younger men have struggled. But there is no shame in being afraid. If you aren't then there is something wrong with you."

The Dragoons have been generally positive about an Army initiative which sees stress counselling offered to soldiers immediately after large battles.

"Nobody wanted to do the meetings," said Corporal Steven Sodeau, 33, the unit medic. "But once we were in there nobody would shut up."

It is a war that men have found easier to justify to themselves than the Iraq war, but they find it hard to know who the enemy are; particularly since irregular militia units roam the country in garb indistinguishable from the Taliban.

"Just because you see some hoods with AKs [AK-47 "Kalashnikov" automatic rifles] and RPGs it doesn't mean that they are enemy," Major Warrack warned his men as they planned an operation west of the provincial capital, Lashkar Gah. "Within minutes of you firing I am answering bloody complicated questions on why you used weapons. I am not saying you can't use them but I need a bloody good explanation if you do."

On several occasions Taliban fighters have taken refuge behind civilians to escape Nato fire. The Dragoons have been kept under observation by Taliban fighters who have put women in their cars to prevent the British soldiers engaging them. Nor can the British arrest suspected Taliban who sometimes bury their weapons and walk through British lines as civilians.

"In Iraq people were constantly asking for more, but here they just want to be left alone," said Captain Jake Rugge-Price, 26. Local people tell the British that they have little liking for the Taliban, but their loyalties are hard to gauge.

"80% of these people support the Taliban. None of them like Nato forces," claimed one of the Dragoons' local interpreters.

The issue of drugs remains a stumbling block. British commanders want nothing to do with the issue, fearing that association with counter-narcotics operations will make it impossible to win popular support.

But simultaneously Britain leads the international effort on counter-narcotics in Afghanistan.

"We are here to help bring development to your area," the Dragoons told locals at checkpoints. "We are nothing to do with poppy eradication."

But many of the local security forces are involved in the drugs trade and other forms of criminality. Local militias have played a major role in recent operations in Helmand, but are loyal to anti-Taliban commanders who are notorious for their involvement in drugs, as are many of the provincial officials the British army must work alongside.

> Most of the Dragoons believe that they will ultimately win the fight against the Taliban. "I feel we have got the upper hand, though at this pace it will be long and drawn out" said WO2 McKenzie, "but we need more fighting troops. There are two support soldiers for every fighting soldier here. *But it is entirely winnable.*"

These engagements had a bonding effect for C Squadron and the brigade. Mutual suspicion was replaced by trust and respect; and for the rest of the tour the squadron's capabilities, flexibility and "can do" approach, meant they were employed on all large-scale operations.[3]

In March 2007 there was another major operation, "Silver", the squadron moving up the east of the Sangin Valley – northeast of Camp Bastion, towards the border with Kandahar province – to interdict and cut off Taliban fighters. More than 1,000 troops from a number of nations took part with the objective of relieving Sangin. In late June 2006, under pressure from President Karzai, the decision had been taken to deploy British troops in Sangin to enforce the authority of the Afghan government, a significant change – at least, for the time being – from the "oilspot" (or "inkspot") strategy that had been tried previously around Lashkar Gah.[4] Nato's Regional Command South (a two-star – major-general's – command comprising the provinces of Nimruz, Helmand, Kandahar, Daykundi, Uruzgan and Zabul), based at Kandahar international airport, gave advance warning of the coming operation through the town elders and by dropping leaflets.

---

3. The non-military reader might be puzzled by the idea of "mutual suspicion". It stems in part from the Marines being a branch of the Navy rather than the Army, and also the condescension of "elite" troops such as they and the Parachute Regiment towards the rest – a tiresome fact of life which the Falklands War alone ought to have put paid to, when both Marines and Paras suddenly discovered the worth of CVR(T) and the professionalism of their crews.
4. The idea – *Tache d'huile* – came from the French General Gallieni's experience in Indo-China in the 1890s: "words meant *nothing* unless combined with a simultaneous work of organization — roads, telegraphs, markets, crops — so that with the pacification there flowed forward, like a pool of oil, a great belt of civilization."

A battalion from the 82nd (US) Airborne Division augmented by elements of the ANA launched heliborne assaults at various locations some five kilometres south of the district centre. On 5 April, coalition troops occupied Sangin, meeting only light resistance, the Taliban having quit the town, as well as most of its inhabitants. Though the Taliban continued to operate in the surrounding areas, the Afghan civil authorities were at least able to return, marking the end of what had effectively been a tight Taliban siege of the district capital. The provincial governor appointed a new local governor, and a permanent ANA base was established.

The operation was indeed a significant success – as far as it went – setting the conditions for the relative peace that was to follow in Sangin for the next six months. The operation was not without its close calls for the squadron, but again they came out unscathed. Lieutenant Townsend-Rose was told that his Scimitar had missed an anti-tank mine by inches. He was heard to comment that "it looked too much like a mine to be a mine", a reverse of the usual understanding of becoming "mine conscious."

In his after-tour review Major Warrack was keen to stress, however, that day-to-day the squadron was not engaging with the enemy, rather using its reconnaissance skills in gathering intelligence. In contrast with the contacts, the work essentially demanded patience: "The conditions in which our soldiers operate are harsh but rewarding. Very little has changed in the way soldiers operate in the desert since the days of Stirling [Lieutenant-Colonel David Stirling, founder of the SAS], and the long-range desert group of the North African campaign in the Second World War. It is hot by day [as much as 50°] and cold by night. Rations continue to be fairly monotonous and sand storms rip through our convoys leaving sand everywhere: you would be amazed where it can get to. But there is something very special about the desert as well. Going to sleep in a good sleeping bag on the desert floor having had your fill of an all-in-one cook-up under the stars is a very satisfying moment. Like all harsh terrains, once drills and skills are worked up to a good level you can actually make life very comfortable."

* * *

Operational honours and awards are a tricky and imprecise area of warfare. Churchill, as ever, perfectly summed up the problem:

> "The object of giving medals, stars and ribbons is to give pride and pleasure to those who have deserved them. At the same time a distinction is something which everybody does not possess. If all have it, it is of less value. There must, therefore, be heartburnings and disappointments on the borderline. A medal glitters, but it also casts a shadow. The task of drawing up regulations for such awards is one which does not admit of a perfect solution. It is not possible to satisfy everybody without running the risk of satisfying nobody. All that is possible is to give the greatest satisfaction to the greatest number and to hurt the feelings of the fewest."

There is no doubt that the army prefers to err on the cautious side: "less is more", and all that. Nevertheless, Sergeant Wilkinson was mentioned in despatches, Major Warrack received the Queen's Commendation for Valuable Service (QCVS), and SSM Berry and SSgt Ivan Green REME, the squadron "Tiffy" (Artificer – the NCO commanding the squadron's REME section), received Joint Commander's Commendations.

Chapter Four

Herrick 6: April 2007–October 2007

"It is entirely winnable."

16th Air Assault Brigade had been replaced by 3rd Commando Brigade, who had been as eager to get to grips with the enemy as their great rivals the Parachute Regiment had been, if in a different way. They in turn were replaced in April 2007 by 12th Mechanized Brigade, and although the expected spring offensive by the Taliban didn't materialize, almost certainly due to the large number of casualties their foot soldiers had taken in their frontal assaults the previous summer, the tour was just as kinetic. It was on this tour – Herrick 6 – that The Light Dragoons deployed for the first time as a unit, albeit multi-capbadge. In his introduction to the 2007 edition of the regimental journal, which went to print two-thirds of the way through C Squadron's tour, the commanding officer, Lieutenant-Colonel Angus Watson, commented on the preparation for deployment: "The order of battle has changed numerous times over the last few months as the [ISAF] operation develops and matures but currently it is anticipated that we will provide the core of a battlegroup which will operate in the southern half of Helmand province. The key elements of the battlegroup will include B Squadron [five troops], the [squadron-strength] composite brigade recce force (BRF), and Number 3 Company of the Grenadier Guards. In addition, we will expect to take under command a number of other ISTAR assets, because battlegroup headquarters will have a responsibility for the conduct of intelligence collection across the whole of Helmand province for the UK task force. This construct could be regarded as a seminal moment in the development of the formation reconnaissance regiment for the 'Future Army' structure, as we have the opportunity to lead the key business of ISTAR in a complex and challenging operation."[1]

This was indeed a step change: a tactical area of responsibility (TAOR), with in addition the task of province-wide intelligence gathering. The TAOR, based on the Helmand provincial capital of Lashkar Gah (LKG), itself a significant responsibility to be entrusted to the regiment, stretched from LKG some 140 miles to the border with Pakistan – and thus they were designated "Battle Group (South)": BG(S). The Helmand river – and therefore the Green Zone – runs a little over half this distance south before turning west and flowing towards Iran though Nimruz province. However, the focus for BG(S)'s activity was to be exclusively Garmsir district. For if there was ever a definitive front line with the Taliban, it was just south of the district centre, the only significant concentration of population, and where by spring 2007 the majority of the people had moved away thanks to Taliban intimidation. LD's presence was intended to reassure the remaining locals and the small Afghan National Police (ANP) detachment which was responsible for the only bridge over the Helmand River south of Lashkar Gah – and so in routine use by both locals and the Taliban – thus protecting the southern gateway to the ADZ (Afghan Development Zone).[2] "We did this at Garmsir by patrolling out from the Patrol Base DELHI," explained Lieutenant-Colonel Watson in his operational de-briefing on return; "the check points around it were hit regularly, sometimes six or seven times a day. The squadron on the other hand conducted recce-strike operations (finding and striking the enemy when and where they could)."

1. "Future Army" structure: a further and wide-ranging review – cuts – following those at end of the Cold War ("Options for Change", which saw the formation of The Light Dragoons) to try to align its organization with what was seen as the future priority – sustained operations such as those in Afghanistan.
2. ADZs were first secured and then held whilst reconstruction and development effort was put into them in an attempt to demonstrate to the local population that the Government of Afghanistan was making a difference. The ADZ in Helmand Province was essentially Lashkar Gah and Gereshk.

It would also be in preparation for the large US Marines operation and subsequent takeover of the TAOR.

The deployment began officially on 30 March and ended on 26 September. The so-called enduring mission was "to find and disrupt [Taliban] within boundaries in order to deny the enemy the ability to influence the Afghan Development Zone (ADZ)." The original plan had been that British forces would secure the ADZ in Helmand province, a triangle of some 150 square miles between LKG, the economic capital of Gereshk, and the Nad-e-Ali District, before slowly expanding their sphere of influence outwards as security improved. The Department for International Development (DfID), the Foreign and Commonwealth Office (FCO) and other civilian actors charged with reconstruction efforts would move into areas secured by British forces, taking over from the small and under-resourced American PRT. Barely half of 16th Air Assault Brigade's strength had been committed directly to this task, but even if the entire brigade had confined themselves to the ADZ, which they hadn't, the numbers were (and not just with hindsight) insufficient for the task.

Falling out from LD BG's mission were four principal tasks: first, to secure Garmsir; second, to mentor ANP, who in effect were paramilitaries; third, to be prepared to operate in partnership with the ANA; and fourth, to be prepared to provide a sub-unit under tactical command of Battle Group (North) to find and disrupt in the Sangin Valley.[3]

---

3. Tactical Command (TACOM): "the authority delegated to a commander to assign tasks to forces under his command for the accomplishment of the mission assigned by higher authority. Under TACOM the gaining commander may only allocate to the assigned force a specific task consistent for the accomplishment of the mission and purpose assigned by the higher commander, that is, within the parameters of the current mission given by the higher authority. TACOM is used where the superior commander recognizes the need for additional resources for a task but requires the resources intact for a later role. Under TACOM the assigned force is allocated for specific tasks and is allocated normally for a limited period of time. This prevents the gaining commander from employing the assigned force in a role or manner not intended by the higher commander. When the task is complete or the specific timeframe expires, the TACOM relationship with the gaining force ends. TACOM is usually

Lieutenant-Colonel Watson framed his "intent" (or concept of operations) with an eye not just to Herrick 6 but to the longer term: "It is imperative that all elements of BG (S) understand that ultimate success in the campaign can only be achieved if there is coherence between the aims of each period of six months.[4] The principal theme is to FIND. This is not just about locating enemy forces (EF) but also about seeking to understand the complexity of the environment and its people. The second theme is to DISRUPT EF. The focus will necessarily be on kinetic activity as we seek to disrupt and destroy EF, but equally non-kinetic (information operations, psychological operations etc[5]) will also DISRUPT and will be employed in a complementary manner."

Specifically, Lieutenant-Colonel Watson intended expanding the area of influence from Garmsir south by actively clearing the Taliban and then using "non-kinetic effects" to influence local Afghans to try to isolate them from the Taliban who had previously fed from (or preyed on) them. In this he recognized that he would have to use resources outside BG(S), not least ANF.

Training culminated, as in every Herrick rotation, in the mission rehearsal exercise (MRX). As the regimental journal records with some understatement, "the reality of cold, wet training on Salisbury Plain was a long way from what we experienced in Southern Helmand." Heat

---

applied to specific situations and to elements that have unique capabilities." AJP-3: Allied Joint Doctrine for the Conduct of Operations, 2002.

4. In the judgement of the author, who as the Daily Telegraph's and later the Times's military commentator attended most of the successive brigade commanders' post-operational debriefs in the MoD, Lieutenant-Colonel Watson was ahead of the field in thinking thus at the tactical level.
5. Information operations: "Coordinated actions undertaken to influence an adversary or potential adversary in support of political and military objectives by undermining his will, cohesion and decision-making ability, through affecting his information, information-based processes and systems while protecting one's own decision-makers and decision making processes." Psyops: "Planned activities using methods of communication and other means directed at approved audiences in order to influence perceptions, attitudes and behaviour, affecting the achievement of political and military objectives."

resistant paint and an air-conditioning modification would help reduce heat by some 12 degrees in CVR(T) – which probably simply brought the internal temperature down to the ambient average 40 degrees at the height of summer. But in the extremes of temperature – 50 degrees was not uncommon – the extra heat of the engine fed by US aviation fuel rather than the preferred diesel, and labouring with the weight of additional armour, the driver in particular could be subjected to an extreme of 65 degrees – and that with the hatch *open*. When obliged to close down – in some contacts for over eight hours – he could only effectively be cooled by water poured over him by the crew commander. It is remarkable, but fine testament to the fitness and grit of the drivers, as well as the watchfulness of commanders, that the regiment would suffer only two significant heat casualties during the tour.

B Squadron had the great advantage of taking over from fellow Light Dragoons. Major John Godfrey, the squadron leader, described "the relief and emotion on the faces of the C Squadron vehicle commanders as they rolled into camp Bastion at 02:00 hours at the end of their final patrol, leaving us under no illusions as to the demands of the situation the squadron now faces." The handover, some ten days, was intensive, the "Legion" pulling out all the stops to brief B Squadron on all their hard-learned lessons. The vehicle fleet, already six months in theatre and starting to show signs of exhaustion after many thousands of miles across unforgiving terrain, was worked on by the outgoing crews into the small hours each night to make sure it was ready for the change of owners. "Then, with heads still spinning from the G2 [Intelligence] and ground briefs from the C squadron hierarchy, we were off under our own steam for a 48-hour shake-out exercise in the desert. After all the months of training, most of it on the unrealistic heavily wooded setting of Salisbury Plain, it was a joy to get into the open desert and move in formation as a squadron for the first time."

At the end of March, RHQ deployed to Lashkar Gah and took over from 3 Commando Brigade's "Information Exploitation Group", and became formally "Headquarters, Battle Group (South), Task Force

Helmand": HQ BG(S). Throughout the tour all the battlegroups in the brigade operated a flexible order of battle, which allowed sub-units to redeploy to those areas of Helmand where they were most appropriate and most needed. The major sub-units of the BG(S)'s command for much of the tour were B Squadron, Number 3 Company 1st Battalion Grenadier Guards, the brigade reconnaissance force (BRF), and 127 Battery, Royal Artillery, though at times included Estonian armoured infantry, A Company, The Worcestershire and Sherwood Foresters Regiment (WFR) – subsequently, 2nd Battalion, The Mercian Regiment – ANA sub-units and assorted others.

The first combined-arms operation took place towards the end of April in Garmsir, Operation *Megak*, a Grenadier patrol supported by the squadron.

BG(S) – or, to keep the narrative focussed on the regiment, the "LD BG" – conducted two significant combined, joint, and combined-arms[6] operations during the tour that saw BG HQ deploy into the desert in order to command over 700 troops from a variety of multinational sub-units. The first was Operation *Bataka* in June, a combat-bridging operation (deployment of an MGB – medium girder bridge, or, loosely, Bailey bridge) to improve mobility and security in Garmsir district. 30 Field Squadron of 26 Engineer Regiment, Royal Engineers, were tasked with bridging a canal, covered by the LD BG.[7] The sappers were proud to record that this was the first time that such a bridge had been constructed under fire since the Second World War. The operation went to plan despite a 24-hour delay caused by an equipment fault with the vital support helicopters. And the officer commanding

6. "Combined operations" = multi-national. "Joint" = land and air (and sea, if there is any); "Combined arms" = combinations of infantry, mobile protected firepower, artillery, engineers, army aviation etc. (the term "All Arms", as it implies, means every single arm, and is now used principally to refer to such as training, dress or drill that is applicable to every arm of the service).
7. The canal, roughly a kilometre to the east of the river, was one of several throughout Helmand Province built by the Americans in the 1950s and fed by sluice gates at intervals along the Helmand River.

30 Field Squadron won a wager with the brigade commander over the time it would take to complete the construction (won thanks to some outstanding low-level leadership in the engineer squadron and exhaustive rehearsal in the days and nights before the operation).

In his 2016 book *On Afghanistan's Plains: Courage and Compassion on the Front Line*, Barry Alexander, a former Royal Army Medical Corps (RAMC) nursing officer, gives an interesting – and troubling – snapshot of the operation:

> "There were five of us in the medical team that provided support to troops from the Grenadier Guards and the Worcestershire and Sherwood Foresters (WFR) who were tasked with crossing a canal using infantry footbridges and securing a bridgehead on the far bank to cover the Royal Engineers who built a Bailey bridge to enable vehicles to cross the canal and dominate territory that had previously been in enemy hands. The bridge was built at night and at great speed. This was the first time that a Royal Engineers unit had undertaken such a task under combat conditions since the Korean War.
>
> The operation opened shortly before last light with an artillery bombardment from the 105mm Light Guns of 19 Regt, Royal Artillery. This sought to deter the Taliban from mounting any attacks that night. Once the bridge was built, at first light the infantry commenced a clearance operation of the village on the far bank of the canal to dislodge any enemy that remained. As the troops cleared through, a single Taliban fighter was killed; his comrades had fled, leaving behind their weapons and still-hot kettles of water to brew their tchai.
>
> The clearance operation was something of an anti-climax and a relief at the same time. Once the troops had cleared the village, we received orders to return to our base, patrolling back over the newly built bridge. On our return to our base (FOB – Forward Operating Base – Delhi), the artillery once again fired into

known enemy positions. Later that morning, a local man brought two children to the base who had been injured as a result of the artillery bombardment. We treated them and arranged for them to be transported to hospital. To see such horrific injuries inflicted upon small children was sickening, especially considering it was our artillery strikes that had been responsible."[8]

There in a nutshell was the problem of fighting an enemy who moved among the local population.

The second operation was *Chakush* (Hammer), a brigade-level offensive beginning in the early hours of July 24 in the area between Hyderabad and Mirmandab, north-east of Gereshk, designed to continue the momentum of an operation in March, further north in the Sangin Valley, in which C Squadron had taken part, by expelling the Taliban from the Upper Gereshk Valley. Some 1,500 ISAF and 500 ANSF took part.

The operation was more than usually challenging for BG HQ because it was taking place in central Helmand outside the southern area of operations, and also because command troop was a very slimmed down shadow of its normal self due to the cap on troop numbers in-theatre. They also had to improvise a mobile command post in Vikings, derived from the original over-snow personnel carriers (later designated "multi-terrain") rubber-tracked vehicles that D Squadron 13/18H had known in Norway in the 1980s when serving with Nato's Allied Command Europe's Mobile Force (Land) – but now seriously up-armoured and up-engined, as well as having a one-man turret with either a .5 inch-calibre heavy machinegun or a 40mm automatic grenade-launcher.

8. Both the battery commander and LD commanding officer saw the children arrive: "It was indeed a devastating moment," recalled Lieutenant-Colonel Watson, "and one for which training does not really prepare you. And it had an effect on the battery as a whole – observers and gun position – such that they imposed additional steps into the fire mission procedure to prevent its happening again."

In the initial stage of the operation, ISAF and ANSF were to advance to secure a strategic bridge over the Nahr-e-Seraj canal, clearing and searching compounds, before sappers from 26 Engineer Regiment built a joint forward operating base (FOB) to be named "Arnhem". After a period of intensive planning over unfamiliar maps, BG HQ deployed to Camp Bastion to marry-up with those who were to comprise the rest of the battlegroup – principally the Grenadiers' No 3 Company, B Company 1 Royal Welsh, a company of ANA, along with, under various states of command, troops from Estonia, Denmark and the US. B Squadron, however, stayed-put to look after the BG(S) TAOR.[9]

The Royal Welsh made the initial break-in to the Green Zone, followed up by the Grenadiers and the ANA company, who consolidated over the next few days. With the infantry systematically clearing the area, the BRF squadron – Falcon Squadron, 2nd Royal Tank Regiment – in Mastiffs (a heavily armoured, wheeled personnel carrier), and the Estonian armoured infantry company in Finnish-made wheeled APCs and US MaxxPro MRAPs (Mine Resistant Ambush Protected vehicles) securing the flanks[10], the sappers were able to begin construction. After thirteen days the battlegroup was able to handover the completed FOB Arnhem and a large cleared area of the Green Zone to Battle Group (Centre), and withdraw to Lashkar Gah.

---

9. "Intensive planning": BGHQ followed ruthlessly the "combat estimate process" (once known as the "military appreciation"), conducted war-games with all involved, and then held rehearsals on a large map that was constructed by Command Troop and attached RA and RE personnel. "This was immensely valuable and got the BG from Camp Bastion to the assembly area in good order. The move from there on to the FUP [forming-up point] was less ordered; it was a night move of a mixed fleet of tracked and wheeled vehicles over challenging terrain in which some wheeled vehicles got stuck. Consequently H-Hour was delayed by 30 minutes, to my irritation and the consternation of the Gunners!" recalled Lieutenant-Colonel Watson, adding that it all emphasized the value of planning rather than "the plan" (and, suggests the author, the need to keep H-Hour "at my command" rather than conceding it to the Gunners!).
10. Some Estonian troops had earlier fought in Afghanistan as members of the Soviet Army, before Estonia's independence in 1991.

The Taliban had put up considerable resistance, however, and not without cost to ISAF: Guardsman "Jaffa" Atherton of the Grenadiers, and Sergeant Barry Keen of 246 Signals Squadron (Electronic Warfare) were killed during the operation.

The effort in the Gereshk valley would continue with other ISAF troops until early November, by which time a firm frontline south of the Helmand river had been established, and Regional Command South could begin preparing for an attack towards Musa Qaleh, which had been under Taliban control for eight months. It was all "little by little", but it was progress.

Meanwhile, B Squadron in the BG(S) TAOR were developing the technique of "recce strike", which in the past, notably in Malaya and Vietnam when carried out by infantry, had variously been called "search and destroy", "seek and destroy", "search and clear" and the like. The TAOR was dominated by the river Helmand itself, with only one crossing point in over fifty miles and very few for vehicles on the canal to the east. Until Operation *Bataka* put in place the MGB, the enemy always knew when the squadron was out and about. Deploying vehicle-mounted patrols ("mogging") of up to three weeks' duration, the squadron spent the initial month also gaining a feel for the ground and learning from the so-called combat indicators when a fight was likely. Resupply during these long-term patrols was unconventional, at least compared with training for operations in Europe. Patrols carried five days' combat supplies, replenished by the squadron second-echelon which included DROPS (Demountable Rack-Offloading and Pick-up System). Replenishment was by Chinook helicopter or C130 Hercules, and lessons were learned quickly. Fuel in jerrycans could only be airdropped between a third and a half full, so almost twice the number would be dropped than expected. What was then to be done with so many empty jerrycans? And if a Chinook wasn't able to deliver underslung loads, then carefully protected engines and main assemblies could be dropped at night by parachute from the Hercules.

The problem then was extraction of the broken item for refurbishment. It was a time of creative logistical thinking.

Contacts with the Taliban could be at the proverbially long-range of the Afghan *jezailchi* (rifleman; although Afghan marksmanship frequently failed to live up to its advance billing), but equally – and indeed frequently in B Squadron's case – they could be at alarmingly short range: "On more than one occasion callsigns [individual vehicles] were engaged by RPGs and small-arms fire from under 20m range," recalled Major Godfrey. "In these frenzied moments, crews returned fire with personal weapons including SA80, and even hand grenades, until turrets could be brought to bear." On one occasion, "displaying a great sense of humour, a Taliban fighter was observed firing at a crew and laughing hysterically right up to the moment the turret pointed directly at him, whereupon he disappeared again." To which, he added, as many of his CVR(T) gunners must have agreed, "Oh for the speed of a powered rather than a hand-cranked turret!"

In his post-operational report, Lieutenant-Colonel Watson remarks that both 30mm and GPMG coax gunnery techniques ought to be examined in light of the experience of short-range contacts, rather than, as was the case, practice being predominantly at ranges above 600 metres.

Some fire-fights were over in an instant and some raged for hours, with ammunition replenishment hastily arranged between vehicles in contact. In one not unusual four-hour contact the squadron fired some 11,000 rounds of coax and over 400 rounds of 30mm, while the forward air controller directed 500-pound laser-guided bombs, and an Apache attack-helicopter fired Hellfire missiles into several bunkers.

The Desert Hawk mini-UAV (unmanned aerial vehicle – "drone") proved an invaluable addition to the recce armoury, not least as a deception measure. On one occasion it was flown along a 5km length of a Musa Qaleh Wadi to identify suitable exit points, as B Squadron's journal recounts: "A single pass was made over the selected location, but the UAV subsequently flew throughout the night at a lower level over a number of realistic alternatives. The enemy could hear it buzzing overhead and concentrated their efforts on blocking our extraction at these locations. Such an unproven recce was undoubtedly a risk, but one deemed acceptable under the circumstances. When the squadron moved the following morning, the extraction was almost unmolested."[11]

From July until the end of the tour, the squadron was re-tasked to the centre and north of the province, operating directly to brigade headquarters with, successively, the Royal Anglians, WFR and Royal Marines, or alongside 1 Para, the US Marines and the Czech special operations group, as well as with the ANA's recce *kandak* (battalion) trained and mentored by members of D (Command and Support) Squadron.

This mentoring role was of growing importance in building up the fledgling ANA capability, elements of D Squadron deploying with the Grenadiers' operational mentoring and liaison team (OMLT).[12] The mentoring took several forms, ranging from hands-on training in the field to more informal advice sessions in Camp Shorobak (the local ANA brigade's firm base) alongside Camp Bastion, or while deployed in one of the outstations. How much mentoring was possible was in large part determined by the pace of operations and the will of the ANA, which, recalled David Rae, the sergeant-major for the OMLT, was "usually widespread negative", not least on account of absence without leave and drugs consumption, so much so that little effective training could be done while in camp. Accompanying ANA patrols

11. The squadron leader, Major John Godfrey, recalled "We knew that the enemy expected us to extract using routes that had been recced by the DH3 [drone]. By flying once only along the route being recced for the squadron's extraction to confirm suitability, but then repeatedly circling other crossing points over obstacles, we convinced the TB that we would move the following morning on a different route. They waited in ambush for us in the wrong place and our friends from the US SF called in F15 strikes to suppress them while we negotiated the awful terrain out of the area, in a 2 km-long convoy including 4-ton unprotected trucks."
12. The regiment also had a strong presence in Kabul with the ANA NCO Training Team (NCOTT) led by Captain Norman Mustard.

was therefore unpredictable and hazardous. There was always the risk of deliberate fratricide – and during training for the role, mentors were apprised of the "signals", such as they were – but the greater risk was in ANA losing self-confidence. When contacts occurred, troops of whatever rank instinctively turned to their mentors for the lead. Indeed, although the recce *kandak* was officially battalion-size, roughly 600 men, in reality it was never more than a company of standard ANA soldiers. Sergeant-Major Rae summed up the *kandak* grimly but realistically: "They had no recce skills, equipment or capabilities. They were illiterate and could not be taught even the most basic skills such as map reading for them to have any effect as recce. They were Infantry mentored in basic infantry skills by Recce soldiers."

A mountain to climb – and still not into the foothills.

However, the regiment itself was displaying a fine degree of agility, as in late summer two operations in particular perfectly demonstrated. Towards the end of August, B Squadron were deployed to BG(North) on Operation *Palk*. Taliban fighters had been playing havoc with ISAF forces in the area between Musa Qaleh and Sangin, predominantly in the green zone to the east of the Musa Qaleh Wadi. The squadron were ordered to deploy north from Camp Bastion and cross the wadi just south of Musa Qaleh before "finding and fixing" the Taliban in the area between the two towns. US Marine Corps (USMC) units would then flush the wadi and the squadron would be in place to cut off their avenues of escape. After a three-day tactical move over several hundred miles, the squadron were in place on the knife-edged sand and gravel dunes just above Sangin, from which they were able to observe as the Royal Anglians and USMC engaged in a long and protracted contact in and around Sangin, with a number of arrests and interdictions made as Taliban tried to escape. As night approached, 3rd Troop mounted a clearing patrol during which they were able to deceive the Taliban into thinking they would move out the following morning by a different route to that which they intended. The Taliban waited in ambush in the wrong place and US Air Force F15s struck at them while the squadron managed to extricate themselves without loss to direct fire. However, in one of the wadis 3rd Troop leader's Scimitar detonated a Soviet-made TM-72 anti-tank mine. Seven kilograms of military-grade explosive tore through the side of the vehicle, removing the track and four road wheels and scattering debris some 200 yards. All three crew had been "head up", with their body armour, helmets and weapons in the side bins because space was so tight in the turret and driver's seat. They scrambled out deafened, and half-blind due to the smoke and dust. None was bloody, however, although the troop leader, Second-Lieutenant Merlin Hanbury-Tenison, and gunner, Lance-Corporal Mark Foley, were covered in yellow fluid. A shard of metal had sliced through the back bin and shattered a large tub of Colman's English mustard (made not that far from Swanton Morley, in Norwich) kept to flavour the desert rations. Once the troop leader realized they had detonated a mine, he called his other three vehicles up to create a cordon in case of a Taliban follow-up.

On seeing the explosion, the troop sergeant, Steve Mahon, said later that he had been convinced that all three would be dead. Fortunately, however, the squadron had fitted new under-armour two weeks earlier as the IED threat increased. If this hadn't been fitted the crew would not have been so lucky. Even so, callsign "B30" was deemed unrecoverable and the crew spent the following day with the REME removing every item of useable equipment before the "M" (for "mobility")-kill Scimitar – the first M-kill CVR(T) in Helmand – was rendered wholly useless to the Taliban by "friendly fire".[13]

Then in early September, A Company of the Mercians mounted a clearance operation with support from LD BG's ISTAR and fire support assets to drive out Taliban fighters who were periodically harassing the bridge over the Helmand to the south of Garmsir. While the battlegroup's main HQ remained in Lashkar Gah, the commanding

13. Sergeant Foley, as he then was, died in June 2014 when his vehicle overturned during live-firing training on Warcop ranges, Cumbria.

officer and the operations officer, Captain Tim Dalby-Welsh, deployed forward with their opposite numbers from 5th Battalion Royal Regiment of Scotland (5 SCOTS) who were on a recce for Operation Herrick 8. It was just as well, for after crossing the line of departure (formerly known as the "start line") at about 2100 hours, the company made good, if steady, initial progress and with little resistance. At about 0045 hours, however, the southernmost platoon was ambushed at a range of just twenty metres, taking several casualties, two of them very serious, and one, Private Johan Botha, killed. The next three hours saw some of the most ferocious fighting of the tour. Five times the platoon counter-attacked to recover their wounded, some of who lay just a few metres from the enemy. The reserve platoon then attacked in support, during which the platoon sergeant, Craig Brelsford, was fatally wounded. At about 3 a.m. the company commander took the decision to withdraw in order to consolidate and replenish. No superior leaves a man behind without a good deal of agonizing, and it takes a great deal of moral courage to make the decision, even when hoping the fallen comrade might be recovered later. The company commander had discussed the intention with Lieutenant-Colonel Watson, but even so, it was a tough call.

By this time, it was clear that the company would not be able to continue alone. Lieutenant-Colonel Watson summoned B Squadron from FOB Dwyer some 5 miles west of Garmsir and asked for all the brigade assets that could be spared. Two Apache AH, two fast jets and a US Predator armed drone were quickly despatched to observe the site of the ambush and ensure the Taliban did not remove Private Botha's body. In addition a company of US special operations forces returning from an operation to the south were re-tasked and arrived just before first light in six Blackhawk helicopters. Lieutenant-Colonel Watson, with A Company commander, B Squadron leader, the operations officer and the US special forces commander made a rapid plan to recover Private Botha's body. Despite – perhaps even because of – the hasty planning, the recovery operation went off without a hitch,

B Squadron leading to the ambush site, the US special forces providing flank protection, and A Company recovering their own. It had been a long and difficult night, but small-scale as it was, it demonstrated just how agile LD had become: off-the-cuff planning and executing a joint, combined arms and multi-national operation at night and at high tempo.[14]

* * *

The distances routinely covered during the tour by B Squadron to insert an OP screen or conduct a raid were huge – a 250-mile round-trip in one case – with heavy wear and tear on vehicles in the unforgiving terrain. Battle damage was not insignificant either. In addition to 3rd Troop's write-off, an RPG penetrated one Scimitar, and another was seriously damaged by an IED, fortunately all without serious injuries to the crews. Most of the squadron's "A" (armoured) vehicles were hit by small-arms fire at one time or another. It was unquestionably a kinetic tour, even if day-to-day relatively peaceful. In his post-operational report, however, Lieutenant-Colonel Watson was confident of CVR(T)'s effectiveness in the "Strike" role: "Across the battlegroup soldiers have fought with courage and determination against a tenacious, cunning and at times, ferocious enemy, and have prevailed, causing some significant attrition."

Nevertheless, Lieutenant-Colonel Watson also remarked on how CVR(T) was a "notoriously unreliable platform below the turret ring, and soldiers have worked remarkably hard to maintain a magnificent 80% availability or better during the tour."

14. To illustrate the intensity of the fire-fight: the Mercians' platoon commander was awarded the Conspicuous Gallantry Cross, one of his riflemen, Private Luke Cole, who continued to cover a wounded comrade by persistent fire although a bullet had broken his femur, was awarded the Military Cross, as was Sergeant Brelsford posthumously.

B Squadron leader too was loud in his praise not just of his own crews' determination to keep their "waggons" on the road, but also of his fitter section. In total, the squadron's A vehicle fleet had done 56,500 track-miles in the six-months' tour, and "Without this incredible team, the squadron would quite simply have sat in the desert guarding its own VOR [Vehicle Off the Road – ie, unserviceable] vehicle fleet. At the end of each exhausting day, RAC [Royal Armoured Corps] crews settled into a night-time routine that offered some rest and the chance to admin themselves. By contrast, every evening the REME rolled up their sleeves and worked by torchlight through the night to bring the squadron back up to 100% combat effectiveness (CE) the following morning. Indeed our CE figure was unsurpassed by any other sub-unit in theatre and was all the more impressive given that our 30-year-old vehicles were by far the oldest in theatre. Beyond that backbreaking work, REME personnel also routinely repaired vehicles and weapons systems while in contact with the enemy, getting them back into the fight as quickly as possible. Whenever they were needed they were there, even if they had to get there in an unarmoured 4-ton Bedford truck."

Indeed, this symbiotic relationship – LD and REME – was a marked feature of each of the four Herrick tours.

At the end of Herrick 6, Major Godfrey reflected on what had gone into the making of an effective squadron in Helmand. "We were doing what we had trained for on umpteen exercises over the years on Salisbury Plain, in Germany, Poland and Canada, in the vehicles and with the equipment that we needed to get the job done. What more could we have asked for?"

In other words, operational capability is cumulative.

As for any greater satisfaction than simply knowing they had done their duty to the utmost – the professional's creed – Lieutenant-Colonel Watson (later Brigadier and Colonel of the Regiment) added that they could take both comfort and pride in the knowledge that the "lives of ordinary Afghans had been improved, if only by a small degree." It was, as he had said in his pre-deployment concept of operations, a long game, and ultimate success in the campaign could only be achieved "if there is coherence between the aims of each period of six months."

Nevertheless, success had not come without human cost. Six members of BG(S) died during Operation Herrick 6 (and 26 others in the brigade during the tour). None was LD capbadge, but that was more by the grace of God than the Taliban's intent. Major Godfrey and Captain Binnington were mentioned in despatches. Lieutenant-Colonel Watson received the Queen's Commendation for Valuable Services (QCVS). Seven received Joint Commanders' Commendations: Captain Mick Reed, Staff-Sergeant Simon "Tom" Hensellek REME, Sergeant Michael "Billy" Braithwaite, Sergeant Paul Grahame, Corporal Leslie Binns, Lance-Corporal Joe Stamp, Lance-Corporal Adam Hirst. Five received Commander British Forces' Commendations: Captain Tim Dalby-Welsh, Lieutenant Matthew Fyjis-Walker, Staff-Sergeant Mark Dobbs, Sergeant David Gray, Trooper Lee Wilson.

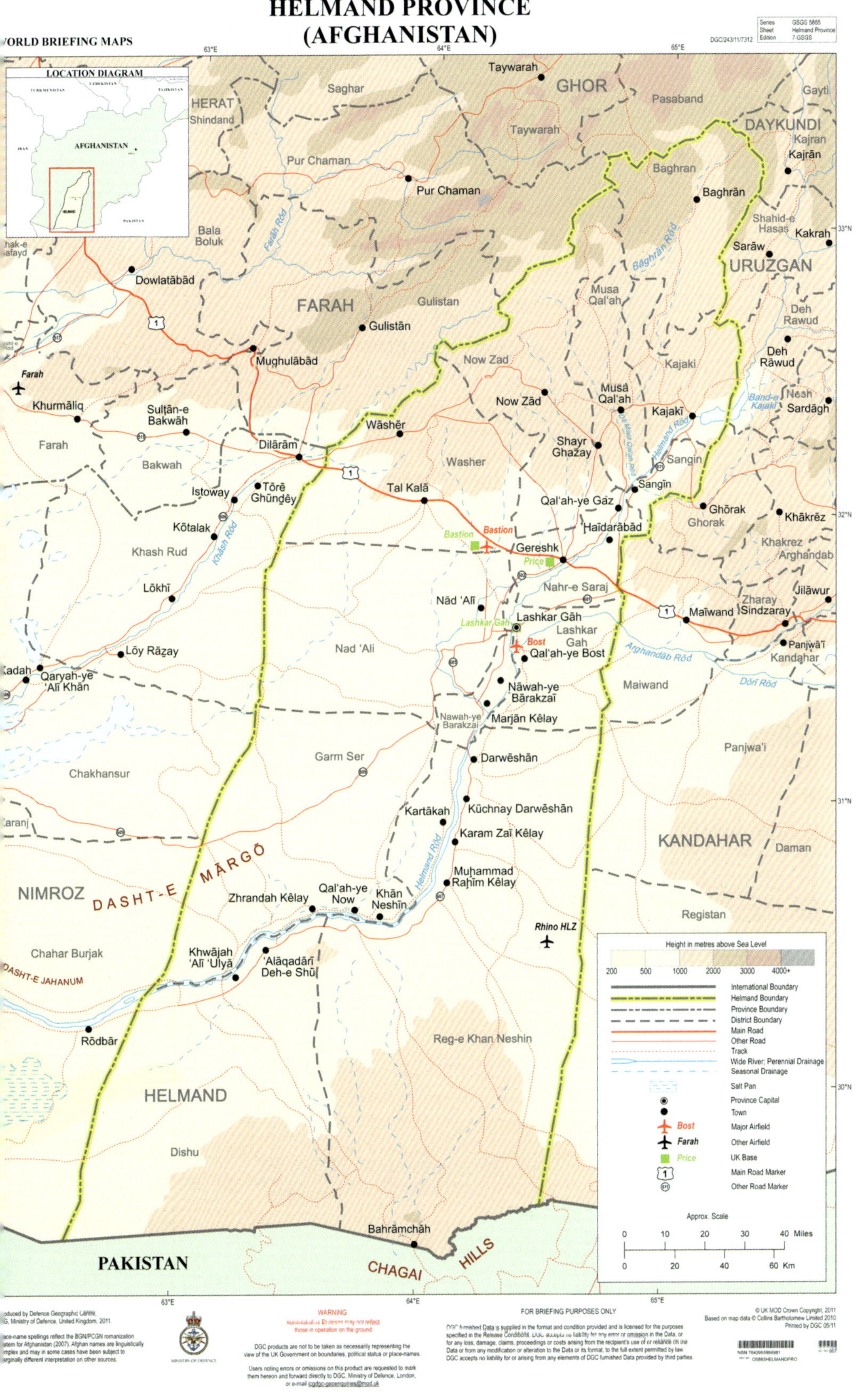

HELMAND PROVINCE
(AFGHANISTAN)
WORLD BRIEFING MAPS
Series GSGS 5865
Sheet Helmand Province
Edition 7-GSGS
DGC/243/11/7312
LOCATION DIAGRAM
AFGHANISTAN
HELMAND
PAKISTAN
63°E
64°E
65°E
33°N
32°N
31°N
30°N
GHOR
HERAT
FARAH
DAYKUNDI
URUZGAN
KANDAHAR
NIMROZ
HELMAND
PAKISTAN
DASHT-E MĀRGŌ
DASHT-E JAHANUM
CHAGAI HILLS
Taywarah
Saghar
Shindand
Pasaband
Gayti
Kajran
Kajrān
Pur Chaman
Baghran
Baghrān
Bala Boluk
Shahid-e Hasas
Kakrah
Sarāw
Dowlatābād
Gulistan
Gulistān
Musa Qal'ah
Baghrān Rōd
Farah Rōd
Deh Rawud
Deh Rāwud
Mughulābād
Now Zad
Now Zād
Kajaki
Kajakī
Farah
Khurmāliq
Sultān-e Bakwāh
Wāshēr
Nesh
Sardāgh
Band-e Kajaki
Bakwah
Dilārām
Washer
Shayr Ghazay
Helmand Rōd
Sangin
Sangīn
Istoway
Tōrē Ghūndêy
Tal Kalā
Qal'ah-ye Gaz
Ghōrak
Ghorak
Khākrēz
Kōtalak
Khash Rōd
Bastion
Haidarābād
Khash Rud
Gereshk
Price
Khakrez
Arghandab
Lōkhī
Nahr-e Saraj
Jilāwur
Nād 'Alī
Lashkar Gāh
Maīwand
Zharay
Sindzaray
Lashkar Gah
Bost
Panjwā'ī
Lōy Rāzay
Nad 'Ali
Qal'ah-ye Bost
Arghandāb Rōd
Kandahar
Qaryah-ye 'Alī Khān
Nāwah-ye Bārakzaī
Dōrī Rōd
Maiwand
Nawah-ye Barakzai
Marjān Kēlay
Darwēshān
Garm Ser
Panjwa'i
Chakhansur
Kūchnay Darwēshān
Kartākah
Karam Zaī Kēlay
Daman
Muhammad Rahīm Kēlay
Zhrandah Kēlay
Qal'ah-ye Now
Khān Neshīn
Registan
Rhino HLZ
Chahar Burjak
Khwājah 'Alī 'Ulyā
'Alāqadārī Deh-e Shū
Rōdbār
Reg-e Khan Neshin
Dishu
Bahrāmchāh
Height in metres above Sea Level
200
500
1000
2000
3000
4000+
International Boundary
Helmand Boundary
Province Boundary
District Boundary
Main Road
Other Road
Track
Wide River; Perennial Drainage
Seasonal Drainage
Salt Pan
Province Capital
Town
Major Airfield
Other Airfield
UK Base
Main Road Marker
Other Road Marker
Approx. Scale
0
10
20
30
40
Miles
0
20
40
60
Km
Produced by Defence Geographic Centre, DGC, Ministry of Defence, United Kingdom, 2011.
Place-name spellings reflect the BGN/PCGN romanization system for Afghanistan (2007). Afghan names are linguistically complex and may in some cases have been subject to marginally different interpretation on other sources.
MINISTRY OF DEFENCE
WARNING
Administrative Divisions may not reflect those in operation on the ground
DGC products are not to be taken as necessarily representing the view of the UK Government on boundaries, political status or place-names.
Users noting errors or omissions on this product are requested to mark them hereon and forward directly to DGC, Ministry of Defence, London, or e-mail icgdgc-geoenquiries@mod.uk
FOR BRIEFING PURPOSES ONLY
DGC furnished Data is supplied in the format and condition provided and is licensed for the purposes specified in the Release Conditions. DGC accepts no liability for any error or omission in the Data, or for any loss, damage, claims, proceedings or costs arising from the recipient's use of or reliance on the Data or from any modification or alteration to the Data or its format, to the full extent permitted by law. DGC accepts no liability for or arising from any elements of DGC furnished Data provided by third parties
© UK MOD Crown Copyright, 2011
Based on map data © Collins Bartholomew Limited 2010
Printed by DGC 05/11

Herrick 5

"We own the desert, but the Taliban own the green areas." C Squadron in the classic role of armoured reconnaissance for 3rd Commando Brigade Group.

"They were to remain as an intact force in the ISTAR (intelligence, surveillance, target acquisition and reconnaissance) role…" which meant dismounted OPs, and the "Mark 1 Eyeball", as well. Trooper Joe Cooperwaite of 2nd Troop.

"…and manoeuvre as a whole in the desert in the southern area of Helmand, uncharted territory." A good position of observation is one that commands a good view, cover in the desert being a secondary consideration.

"...deemed unrecoverable and the crew spent the following day with the REME removing every item of useable equipment". The mine's damage to the hull clearly visible. A large explosive charge finished the job.

"The focus will necessarily be on kinetic activity as we seek to disrupt and destroy EF [enemy forces]". Sergeant Graham Mudd, one of the many augmentees from A Squadron, in sniper role.

"In the initial stage of the operation... clearing and searching compounds". B Squadron searching, the humdrum of any counter-insurgency operation, but always risky.

"At first light, the Light Dragoons battlegroup crossed the line of departure." Operation Panther's Claw, the break-in.

> *The new US commander in Afghanistan, General Stanley McChrystal, brought in by President Obama for his understanding of the complexities of counter-insurgency, puts it simply: "We are fighting for the population." The August elections for the presidency and the Provincial Council representatives are important in this fight for the population, and the aim of Operation Panther's Claw is to clear the Taliban from the heavily populated area between Gereshk, the economic hub of Helmand, and Lashkar Gah, the provincial capital, to allow the Afghans a chance to vote.*
>
> *The Daily Telegraph*, 22 July 2009

Compound clearance in the first few days of Panther's Claw.

"The vegetation provides cover for the Taliban while narrow tracks and concentrations of walled houses slow the Scimitars and funnel them into potential ambush sites." Opportunities for concealing IEDs, too.

Panther's Claw: Scimitar and dismounted Light Dragoons in mutual support.

"By 14 July the Light Dragoons battlegroup were nearing their final objective, a line from the Nahr-e Bughra canal south and east to the Helmand river".

"Brigadier Radford told the battlegroup to pause in Malgir area to recuperate and resupply".

"By 27 July Babaji itself was secured. Intelligence estimated that in all some 200–300 Taliban had been killed, out of perhaps some 500 active in the Green Zone".

Morale: "I remember the extraordinary professionalism, competence and the sheer courage of those young men." US General Stanley McChrystal, speaking of Panther's Claw.

"We will deploy to Helmand at an exceptionally exciting and important time. Transition of security responsibility to the Afghan National Security Forces is of central importance to the UK's timely cessation of combat operations." Transition in action: Light Dragoons and ANSF.

"Very little has changed in the way soldiers operate in the desert since the days of... the long-range desert group of the North African campaign." A troop of A Squadron Jackals leaguered-up for all-round defence. The Jackal would subsequently become the regiment's prime recce vehicle in its new role as "light cavalry" in the Army's "Future Force 2020" concept.

The final evolution: for Herrick 15 the regiment was equipped with Scimitar Mark 2. Each CVR(T) variant was "re-hulled" to give better mine-blast protection, with modified running gear, improved armour added, mine-blast protection seating, repositioned foot controls, revamped fuel system, and anti-roll bar (an in-theatre modification) – in addition to previous upgrades in power output, new gearboxes and transmissions, air-conditioning, improved communications, air filters and night-vision systems.

"A few days later the squadron took part in a helicopter assault to block the Taliban in the Upper Gereshk Valley..." The Chinook: troop-carrier, combat supplies replenisher, vehicle recoverer, lifesaver.

"The Afghan was famed for his long-range sniping; now he'd also become adept at the indirect method, the threat underfoot – mines, some retrieved from the Soviet era, some home-made, the IEDs." This and the illustrations on the cover and endpapers are by the Yorkshire-based artist Lynne Moore, who was "embedded" with the regiment during Herrick 15.

The MoD (Army) website describes The Light Dragoons as "multi-skilled soldiers – fast, adaptable and leading from the front." On successive Herricks they proved at home either mounted or dismounted, with a variety of vehicles, nationalities and species.

Chapter Five

Herrick 10: May 2009–October 2009

"A tenacious, cunning and at times, ferocious enemy"

By 2008, then, the rotational and by now hugely augmented British brigades for Helmand – which once in-theatre were known as Task Force Helmand (TFH) – were training primarily with the expectation of intense combat in up to brigade strength, rather than of work under the original Reid vision that "our mission is not counter-terrorism" but one of "reconstruction." Successive TFHs certainly continued to take casualties, if nothing like the numbers the Taliban had suffered in 2006, and these were beginning to tell with public opinion and therefore political confidence at home. By 2009 the number killed in action in Afghanistan since the first intervention in 2001 was approaching 200. In cold statistical terms this was hardly alarming; during the three and a half decades of Operation Banner (Northern Ireland, 1969–2007), some 1,400 servicemen had died, over half of them in IRA attacks (most of the rest in operational and training accidents), and in the Falklands War of 1982, 250 servicemen died in just over six weeks. Yet proportional to the numbers deployed, the figures were troubling, not least because serious (life-changing) casualties were also increasing alarmingly, as was their public profile. These casualties, usually involving amputations, sometimes of more than one limb, were almost always the result of IEDs, and ten years earlier would likely as not have resulted in death. The increased survival rate was testimony to the remarkable first-aid expertise of the troops on the ground, which had undergone a revolution in the previous decade, as well as to the

RAF's skilful and fearless helicopter casualty evacuation ("casevac"), the trauma surgery and nursing at the main base of British forces in Helmand – Camp Bastion – and subsequently the RAF's medical flights to England, with casualties often in an induced coma.

In the public mind, these grave injuries came on top of the nearly 200 deaths in Iraq, a campaign that had gone badly wrong.[1] And without doubt the sometimes brave but faltering British performance in that insurgency had stung the army's leadership into wanting out as fast as possible in order to restore self-confidence and reputation in what appeared to be a more straightforward if bloody tactical challenge in Afghanistan. Commanders on the ground in Helmand were in no mood to give any impression of unwillingness to get to grips with the enemy, as had sometimes appeared evident in Iraq. And because there was no permanent two-star (division equivalent) headquarters to give consistency and continuity to the campaign, with complete brigades rotating every six months rather than the headquarters staying put while the constituent units came and went in rotation – a departure from all previous counter-insurgency practice[2]

1. Also called the Second Gulf War (2003–11), the conflict consisted of two phases. The first was a brief, conventionally fought campaign (March–April 2003), in which a combined US–British force (with token contingents from several other countries) invaded and rapidly defeated Iraqi military and paramilitary forces. The second phase, the US-led occupation, faced an unexpected (or unexpectedly large) insurgency, which was not quelled until 2007, after which the US and Britain gradually reduced their military presence.
2. The reason given by the then CGS, Sir Richard Dannatt, was that because brigades had to mount brigade-size operations, they had to train as brigades prior to deployment, thus making it unfeasible for their individual units to "trickle" rotate. The reason why command was not vested in a fully functioning permanent two-star headquarters is still a mystery. The key decision-makers in the process weren't army and could see no need for it; and the political imperative of limited liability trumped what was perceived as army 'gold-plating'. The numbers had become the strategy. The result was a brigade headquarters of over 200 strong – a divisional headquarters in all but name – facing a command challenge that was too great. Without a headquarters above them looking upwards and outwards, brigade commanders were too often distracted from the tactical-level fight on which they should have been focusing. As a result, TFH too often lacked focus and agility at the tactical level.

– TFH commanders themselves were naturally focused on shorter-term offensive operations at brigade level. This was the time of the making of names – "seeking the bubble reputation in the cannon's mouth." And why not? For reputation – individual, regimental, army and national – was an implicit, and sometimes explicit, part of the mission. Unfortunately, it didn't conduce to coherence and consistency in the campaign.

That said, there was no want of thoughtfulness at the head of TFH. Indeed, the commander of Herrick 6, Brigadier (later Lieutenant-General Sir) John Lorimer, had read Arabic and Islamic Studies at Cambridge, and in 2018 would become defence senior advisor for the Middle East, an appointment which, if closer to home than Afghanistan, acknowledged at least a marked degree of cultural awareness. But the situation at the beginning of each six-month tour was as he and others found it, and for the most part they could only make the best of a bad job.

By the middle of 2008, with the situation not improving, the commander of Herrick 9, Brigadier Gordon Messenger, whose Royal Marines were expending a good deal of ammunition in many a fire-fight, evidently considered it was time for a rethink. Although the original plan in the spring of 2006, developed by ISAF headquarters and encouraged by the Afghan government (notably President Karzai), had been to focus on the population centres, British forces had got drawn into the "platoon house [Rorke's Drift] strategy", and General Richards in Kabul had only with some difficulty been able to pull them out of it. But General Richards had left Kabul in February 2007, and the US General Dan McNeill had taken his place. His approach was decidedly more aggressive, and McNeill's own successor in June 2008, General David McKiernan, also American, was no less inclined to the mailed fist.

Perhaps being a Royal Marine, though, Brigadier Messenger could take a step back from what might have been perceived as "army" strategy and think afresh.[3] In any event, he concluded that the strategy was flawed, and persuaded both London and the Nato chain of command in Afghanistan to return to the original (Richards) concept of focusing on the centres of population rather than the peripheries – in the case of Helmand, the so-called Afghan Development Zone, the triangle formed by the provincial capital Lashkar Gah, Gereshk (the economic hub of Helmand) and Camp Bastion, twenty miles north-west of Lashkar Gah. This, however, needed more troops than Brigadier Messenger actually had, and he was only able to put a battle group into Nad-e Ali on the other side of the Helmand river west of Lashkar Gah by asset-stripping elsewhere. He was also keen to make their presence less kinetic: "Our reaction to being fired on is still to react in kind, sometimes disproportionately, alienating sections of the population as a consequence," the very thing that British commanders had been critical of the Americans doing, in Afghanistan as well as earlier in Iraq.

Brigadier Messenger's intentions would be endorsed by his successor in the summer of 2009, Brigadier Tim Radford, commanding the 19th Light Brigade. Brigadier Radford, described by one not uncritical defence correspondent as "soft-spoken and cerebral",[4] brought to the campaign a politics degree as well as a special forces background and the accumulated experience of the Northern Ireland "Troubles", Iraq, and a spell as assistant director of counter-terrorism in the MoD.[5] The rotation to Herrick 10 – in which The Light Dragoons would play a prominent and bruising part – also coincided with a change of command in ISAF: in June, President Obama, frustrated by the lack

3. Messenger hadn't been intended for the job, but was hastily transferred from the operations directorate of the MoD when the brigade commander was almost killed in an accident during pre-deployment leave. He'd also been involved in the initial planning for Helmand while serving in the Permanent Joint HQ at Northwood, just outside London.

4. Toby Harnden, *Dead Men Risen* (London, 2011).

5. As a four-star general, Radford would in 2020 become Deputy Supreme [NATO] Allied Commander Europe (DSACEUR), and Messenger Vice-Chief of the Defence Staff in 2016. Helmand was a proving ground for a generation of senior officers.

of progress and encouraged by his Defense Secretary, Robert Gates – who, unusually, had continued in post from the previous administration of President George W. Bush – removed General McKiernan and appointed instead a special forces officer, General Stanley McChrystal.

Steeped in counter-insurgency theory and practice, General McChrystal quickly reset the thinking: "We are fighting for the population and that involves protecting them both from the enemy and from unintended consequences of our operation." He coined the term "courageous restraint" to characterize the approach he wanted.

London too knew that things weren't working. TFH wasn't just a brigade but a civil–military mission coordinating the UK's so-called "comprehensive approach." The civil side operated under the lead of the Foreign and Commonwealth Office (FCO), with the Department for International Development (DfID) and its PRTs trying desperately to work "normally" and with minimal military profile. Indeed, DfID personnel had frequently been reluctant to engage with the counter-insurgency side of the comprehensive approach. By early 2009, senior British officers were increasingly voicing concern that the FCO and DfID "didn't quite have the equation right", that better security was needed to protect the Afghans' reconstruction and governance; and for that, more troops were needed. Parliament voiced concern, too, but with a slightly different emphasis, disturbed that there was "too much kinetic activity going on" and concluding that "they needed to see the evidence of reconstruction and development ... [which was] what the government has presented to the British people."[6]

In April, a report entitled *UK Policy in Afghanistan and Pakistan: A Way Forward* confirmed London's commitment to the counter-insurgency strategy, focusing on Lashkar Gah and other population centres in Helmand, including Gereshk; but the comprehensive, civil–military effort just wasn't getting results. Indeed, in July the House of Commons foreign affairs committee concluded that "the security

6. See Jeffrey Dressler, *Afghanistan Report 2* (Washington DC, 2009).

situation [in Helmand] is preventing any strengthening of governance and Afghan capacity" and that the "security situation makes it extremely difficult for civilians to move around the province, and as a result civilian projects suffer". In other words, to stabilize Helmand and improve security, British forces needed to go all out on combating the insurgency.

Winning the population ought to have been like pushing at an open door, for by and large the Taliban were hated.[7] That much had always been understood; but the door was easily jammed. Indeed, at worst it could actually swing back and close for good if tactical methods continued to kill large numbers of ordinary Afghans, however inadvertently. In other words, reliance on heavy ordnance, particularly aerial bombing, no matter how precision-guided, wasn't an option – not of first resort, certainly. Troops on the ground would have to close with the enemy and be tactically discerning – "courageous restraint."

In this fight for the population, and for the whole nation-building project, 2009 would therefore be a – perhaps *the* – defining year. The elections for both the presidency and the national and provincial councils taking place in August were fundamental to the project. If these were to have any chance of success, in Helmand in particular, it wouldn't be enough simply to guard the polling stations; the Taliban would have to be ejected from the province so that Afghans – an estimated 80,000 in TFH's area of operations – would be able to move freely to and from them. Thus an ambitious operation would be launched in the two months prior to polling, both to clear out the Taliban and to allow the ANSF to occupy and hold the ground, thus linking the provincial capital with the economic capital, which had

7. Notwithstanding Tom Coghlan's assertion that one of the regiment's interpreters had said, "80% of these people support the Taliban. None of them like Nato forces". The problem arose where local governors and "warlords" abused their power, and the Taliban opposed them, seeming thus to be on the ordinary Afghan's side – and, critically, when ISAF forces appeared to be on the side of the oppressors. The problem was of course made worse by Afghans pursuing illegal activities, not least poppy growing, and resenting the intrusion of "authority".

hitherto been “bandit country”. It would take the codename Panther’s Claw – in Pashtun, *Panchai Palang* – and would be carried out by Brigadier Radford’s brigade, due to arrive in theatre in May.

As planning began at the 19th Brigade’s headquarters in Northern Ireland, long before deployment, there were indications of another Taliban offensive against Lashkar Gah. Intelligence reported that Mullah Omar, the Taliban’s leader, intended making Helmand the focus of his main effort, and that several hundreds of Taliban fighters would assault the provincial capital from the north-west and from Marjah across the Bolan desert to the south-west, and mount rocket attacks against the brigade base. Brigadier Radford’s staff therefore began planning to clear the area of Babaji and the so-called Chah-e Anjir Triangle (CAT) – roughly equilateral, 5 miles a side – to strengthen the security of the provincial capital. Any threat to Lashkar Gah had to be taken seriously, for obvious political as well as military reasons. Besides, Helmand’s governor, Gulab Mangal, had for months been pressing Kabul for additional ANA troops. Any provincial governor’s position at this time was precarious, to say the least, and while it was inconceivable that the Taliban could actually capture the town, let alone hold it, any disruption to daily life might make Mangal look weak. (His own compound would be within range of Taliban rockets fired from the Bolan bridge across the Helmand river). President Karzai eventually sent two more *kandaks* to the province.

If Mangal felt there was strategic pressure on his position as governor, British officers – from commanders in Afghanistan to the most senior in Whitehall – most certainly felt the pressure too. Iraq had not been the army’s finest hour. Subtle and effective in the initial capture of Basra in the south, the divisional-size force had rapidly got out of its depth in the subsequent Shia insurgency. It wasn’t so much the fault of the troops on the ground (although the lack of operational “grip” was at times very marked, with the many acts of heroism, including one meriting the award of a VC, marred by acts of thuggery) as the effects of the confusion in the interconnecting corridors of political and military power in London. In particular, the withdrawal from the city of Basra itself to the security of the airport, though well conducted tactically, was little short of a strategic disaster in terms of British relations with US commanders. However much it was presented as "tough love", forcing the Iraqi security forces to take responsibility for the city, it was impossible to counter the impression – the accusations indeed – that the army had pulled out because they weren't prepared to shed blood, and then had to be bailed out by Americans coming down from Baghdad. Or, as one senior American special forces officer put it, "The British wrote cheques they couldn't cash."

The fact was that those at the top in London – particularly in the MoD – had decided that Iraq was unwinnable. They'd not expected to face an insurgency, troop morale was now suffering, and external support was disappearing. But cutting and running from Iraq couldn't be an option unless there was something else to focus on, in a sense to redeem the army's reputation as being competent and willing to fight – in other words, its reputation in the eyes of the public, Whitehall (the Treasury especially), and the world; and in particular the Americans, the military partnership with whom was at the heart of security policy. Afghanistan in 2006 had seemed to offer just that opportunity – a smaller-scale affair well suited to recent British experience of "operations other than war", notwithstanding the bloody noses in Basra. The last thing Brigadier Radford needed now, three years later, as he planned for Herrick 10 was the threat of General McKiernan, who was then still in post, sending US troops in large numbers into Helmand to "kick ass", giving the impression that the Brits couldn't cope – the impression of another Basra.

Herrick 10 also coincided with something of a sea-change in the approach to the campaign in London. Frustrated with Whitehall's – not least the MoD's – view that Afghanistan was just one of a number of continuing commitments (one that just happened to be uniquely bloody), an "operation" rather than a war, General David Richards, by then the army's commander-in-chief, and later to become Chief of the General Staff and then Chief of the Defence Staff, persuaded the MoD that the army needed to be put on what he termed an "operational footing", focusing almost entirely on counter-insurgency, to get fully to grips with the campaign. At first he'd wanted to call it a "war footing", but that was judged a foot too far. But with "Operation Entirety", as it was called, Richards gave notice that the army had to move into a much higher gear.

This, too, would have its effect in shaping Panther's Claw – the sense of at last having some proper "top cover" at home (although, as it would prove, still not enough). As also would the belated realization by the prime minister, Gordon Brown, that under-resourcing the campaign from the outset was now having awkward political consequences.

To begin with, the 19th Light Brigade's order of battle would be larger than hitherto, consisting of a tracked armoured reconnaissance regiment (Light Dragoons) and five infantry battalions – 1st Welsh Guards, 3rd Royal Regiment of Scotland (Black Watch), 2nd Royal Regiment of Fusiliers and 2nd and 4th Rifles, with in addition elements of 2nd Battalion Mercian Regiment and 2nd Battalion Royal Gurkha Rifles as mentoring teams with the ANA and police, together with an armoured infantry company of the 2nd Royal Welsh and strong artillery and engineer support. Also, directly supporting the brigade, as they had its predecessors, would be the Army Air Corps' Apaches and an RAF squadron of Chinook heavy-lift helicopters, with the joint (RN/RAF) Harrier force at Kandahar airfield on call.

However, it was only in February, just two months before deploying, that The Light Dragoons' new commanding officer, Lieutenant-Colonel Angus (Gus) Fair DSO, was given his firm tasking. In addition to providing men for the brigade recce force (BRF) squadron, the regiment were to supply the command element (and an OMLT) of an ad hoc infantry company, provide two half-squadrons of CVR(T), troops to the BRF's tactical air control parties (TACPs) and the Camp Bastion Support Unit, plus several other detachments. Lieutenant-Colonel Fair knew that BGHQ and A Squadron would only be spending a couple of months in Garmsir as BG(S), but the timing and precise location of subsequent tasks (in effect, Operation Panther's Claw) were yet to be confirmed.

The area of operations for Operation Panther's Claw – that is, the battlefield – was compact enough: an area about the same size as the Isle of Wight, but complex – a wedge-shaped plain some 24 miles long from Lashkar Gah in the south to Gereshk to the north-east. Bounded by the Nahr-e Bughra canal on the north side and the Helmand river on the south, it was some 14 miles wide at its south-western end (its southern border formed more or less by the Shamalan canal north-west of Babaji – although the CAT is immediately to the west of the canal), tapering to just a couple of miles at its north-eastern tip. It was an ancient, exceptionally fertile district, a place of open fields and irrigation channels, the Green Zone, with those who farmed the land and tended their animals living in traditional, square-built *qalʿah*s (fortresses). It was certainly not an empty space, and it had been under Taliban control for years, their corridor for operations along the Helmand river. However, the Taliban didn't wear uniforms, and they'd advanced from their earlier strategy of suicidal frontal assaults. The Afghan was famed for his long-range sniping; now he'd also become adept at the indirect method, the threat underfoot – mines, some retrieved from the Soviet era, some home-made, the IEDs. The effect of these wasn't just physical but psychological. Troops in Helmand in particular had become very IED-conscious, both on foot and in wheeled APCs. The IED threat wasn't new, as those who'd served in the border areas of Northern Ireland during the Troubles could testify – and there were still a few. But in South Armagh the IEDs had been "command detonated": an IRA man at the end of a long length of buried cable, or with an electronic device, initiating the explosion. On the whole the IRA were keen to minimize casualties among a civilian population who in those parts were largely sympathetic; but also, they didn't want to waste their resources. Booby traps were rare, therefore. In Helmand the Taliban used command detonation, but also – like the Viet Cong in Vietnam – pressure-plates and tilt-switches, having warned the local population to keep clear.

In the two months preceding 19th Light Brigade's arrival in theatre, the 3rd Commando Brigade (on their second tour within eighteen months) carried out a number of preliminary operations to take and hold ground to give Brigadier Radford's troops a better chance of success. Notable was a four-day action to establish a checkpoint on a key route into Lashkar Gah which would then be manned by Afghan forces mentored by the British to prevent infiltration and to disrupt any spoiling attack the Taliban might make once Panther's Claw was under way. It represented an unusual degree of cooperation, overlap and continuity between brigades.

Brigadier Radford's brigade began arriving in early April, and at once started the delicate job of taking over the ANSF mentoring responsibilities. They had two months in which to refine the plans made at home, to gather more intelligence and adjust to changing circumstances, and to accustom the troops to Helmand. Their final exercise on Salisbury Plain in freezing, snowy January had been as realistic as ground and climate allowed – the Green Zone would have fitted comfortably into the dimensions of the training area, though the plain in winter snow wasn't the Green Zone in summer – and reading the actual ground and its people takes time.

The Light Dragoons were fortunate to return initially to Garmsir as BG(S), to ground they and much of the remainder of the battlegroup had left only eighteen months before. They found a relative haven of tranquillity, as the commanding officer wrote, "a remarkable improvement in the situation. Where there had been poppy now grew wheat, the previously destroyed and deserted bazaar was rebuilt and in constant use, and the school and hospital were refurbished and functioning well under the control of the Afghan departments of Education and Health respectively." Some 15,000 Afghans lived within the TAOR, protected by the battlegroup and "some genuinely excellent ANSF elements."

A Squadron, with their mix of Jackal[8] and CVR(T) took over FOB Dwyer from the commando brigade's BRF, and soon settled into a routine of patrolling in both the desert and the Green Zone, and occasional battle group quick-reaction force (QRF) tasks. However before undertaking its first major operation, deploying a grouping on a seven-day patrol to Lashkar Gah in support of the Welsh Guards (1WG), C Squadron had re-formed to provide two demi-squadrons: "Assaye Troop", comprising two sabre troops, a slimmed-down SHQ, and fitter section, were to be the force reserve (FR); "Emsdorf Troop", comprising 2nd and 4th Troops, were to be attached to A Company 2 Mercian, a light-role infantry company, in a dismounted – ie infantry – role.[9] The reason for this was that as C Squadron were to conduct dismounted tasks for which they were untrained, the commanding officer switched a platoon from A Company to come under command of the squadron. To compensate, he switched in turn two of the squadron's four mounted troops to A Company. This switch was at relatively short notice, and Emsdorf Troop were given six weeks to brush up – or acquire – their infantry skills, which included training with 2 Mercian at Ballykinler in Northern Ireland. Then on arrival in Helmand they were given a troop's worth of CVR(T) in order to offer A Company both a dismounted half-platoon and a mounted troop depending on how they wanted to employ this unique organization.[10] A Company were based in FOB Delhi to provide security and normality for the

8. The Jackal or MWMIK ("Mobility Weapon-Mounted Installation Kit"): one of a family of vehicles designed and developed by Supacat Ltd of Devon for the primary role of deep reconnaissance, rapid assault and fire support (and also used widely in AFG for convoy protection).
9. On formation of The Light Dragoons by the amalgamation of the 15th/19th and the 13th/18th Hussars, C Squadron Light Dragoons continued the tradition of "The Legion", and therefore the demi-squadrons, appropriately, took the name of the 15th/19th's antecedents' singular battle honours, Emsdorf and Assaye respectively.
10. It is worth noting that until the reorganizations of the 1990s, each squadron of an armoured reconnaissance regiment had a support troop – sixteen or so men for dismounted tasks, including demolitions and minelaying.

local population in order to deepen the Afghan authorities' hold within Garmsir District's centre. Emsdorf Troop's tasks were, firstly, to assist the company in its routine "framework" patrolling, whether mounted or dismounted; secondly, to be prepared to assist in company "surge" operations, and thirdly to provide men on a rotational basis for two fixed observation posts (OPs). They were busy.

As, too, were Assaye Troop, who found themselves in demand by the various battle groups. They lost one of their Scimitars early to a legacy mine – one from the era of the Soviet invasion (whether laid by the Soviets or lifted by the Taliban and laid subsequently) – which seriously injured Trooper Matthew Allaway (though he returned to duty and served on until 2012), and when under command of the Welsh Guards in Nad-e-ali, Lance-Corporal Michael Souter was wounded by AK47 fire. After a period of recovery in Camp Bastion, Lance-Corporal Souter returned to the field.

What remained of C Squadron – in effect the core of SHQ under Major Sam Plant – became the command and administrative headquarters of FOB Keenan in the village of Zumberlay in the Upper Gereshk Valley (East), which was variously occupied by elements of 2nd Mercians, 2nd Rifles and the Welsh Guards, and all within the Danish battle group's TAOR. It would later become besieged by IEDs when the mutually supporting FOB Gibraltar was closed in order to reinforce the effort for Panther's Claw. The Taliban, sensing it was their victory, doubled-down on Keenan. Ten soldiers of various capbadges, including four ANA, were killed during this offensive and the reassurance patrols that continued throughout, though none were Light Dragoons. For his handling of the Taliban's IED offensive, Major Plant would be awarded the MBE (Military).

On 30 May, Lance-Corporal Nigel Moffett, detached from C Squadron to the BRF, was taking part in an operation in Musa Qaleh, scouting a route for his troop, when he was killed in action. It was the first loss the regiment had sustained on operations since 1996 in Bosnia. It was not just a loss for the regiment but for the BRF. Lance-

Corporal Moffett had volunteered to join the BRF, which was selected from across all the units of the brigade and had quickly established himself as the fittest member of the force. As a PT instructor he was responsible for running much of the pre-deployment fitness training and brought to the BRF a flare for reconnaissance work and long-range communications, as well as operational experience from Herrick 5. He had fought bravely in several engagements, beginning with an advance against a Taliban stronghold on 23 April. The officer commanding the BRF testified to his soldierly qualities: "He was courageous under fire, and showed a streak of tenacity of which we in the BRF are immensely proud. A committed professional with burning ambition, he was hoping to attempt Special Forces selection next summer after this tour. He would have acquitted himself well."

In another action, Corporal Leslie Binns was blinded in one eye in an IED strike that killed three ANA soldiers, and for his action in the follow up was awarded the Queen's Commendation for Bravery. In 2022 he would reach the top of Everest, having been close to doing so four years earlier when instead he abandoned the attempt in order to tend an injured climber.

In June the regiment handed over the BGS(S) TAOR to a battalion of the US Marine Corps. "For some who had fought over the ground previously it was surprisingly emotional," wrote the second-in-command, Major Hugo Willis. The incoming Marines refused to allow the regiment to haul down the Union flag and said that it would remain flying over FOB Delhi as a symbol of all that UK troops had achieved and sacrificed in that area. "Sometimes, Brits are too cynical and we could learn from our US cousins," added Major Willis. Having handed over to the Marines, the battle group withdrew briefly to Camp Bastion, relocating to FOB Price for Panther's Claw, with BGHQ splitting into Main and Tac for the operation.

Meanwhile, Brigadier Radford had been trying to get the measure of the ANA and police commanders, and the allied contingents, as he would also have under command the Danish battle group, with a troop of German-made Leopard II tanks and an integrated Estonian recce platoon. At the same time, his commanding officers had to turn the concept of operations they'd understood before deployment into concrete plans once they'd accustomed themselves to the ground and the threat. Some would be distinctly troubled by what they saw – especially the mismatch between demands for helicopters and their availability. There was unlikely to be more than a battalion's-worth of lift at any one time, and although the operation would be sequenced ("phased"), with the helicopters switched between the battlegroups, the logistic needs remained. Resupply would therefore have to be by road, which was both dangerous and slow. Helicopters had indeed become a political issue at home, with mounting accusations that the Treasury had cut procurement funding.[11] There was also a complete lack of surveillance equipment covering the approaches to the FOBs, which meant the Taliban had an easier job planting IEDs under cover of darkness. Nevertheless, the operation would have to begin in June to have any chance of clearing out the Taliban and then consolidating the gains before the August elections. Like those planning for D-Day who knew they didn't have all the landing craft they'd like, Brigadier Radford and his staff had to make a plan for Panther's Claw with the resources they were given.

Several more months of intelligence gathering by special forces and the BRF, especially from Afghans displaced from the Green Zone by both the Taliban and fear of the fight to come, and who were now in refugee camps, proved even more valuable than expected. In many respects local knowledge was still poor, however, for despite being in the province since 2006, TFH hadn't been able to immerse itself as deeply as classic counter-insurgency theory prescribed – a consequence of the six-month rotation. One unexpected bonus, however, was the cooperation of a US Marine Task Force, some 4,000 strong, which

11. The Treasury had effectively cut the defence budget in 2003/4, and the (joint) chiefs of staff chose to cut much of the funding for the future helicopter programme.

General McKiernan had ordered south before his sudden departure. Originally intent on an aggressive operation of their own, they were persuaded by Brigadier Radford to deploy instead west of the Helmand river to cover Lashkar Gah from diversionary Taliban attacks.

In essence, Panther's Claw was a cordon and search – or cordon and clear (or even destroy) – operation, a type the British army knew well from many a campaign, but on a new scale and against unprecedented odds, particularly the IEDs. And against an enemy who was expecting it, and was more determined to resist than escape. "Hammer and anvil" comes to mind. The first phase of the operation, to get the cordon (or anvil) in place, began in the early hours of 19 June, with special forces inserted by helicopter to eliminate known Taliban commanders. Soon afterwards, four companies of the 3rd Scots (Black Watch), some 350 men, flew from Camp Bastion in ten US and RAF Chinooks to secure key crossing points of the Nahr-e Bughra canal prior to a direct assault on a Taliban-controlled drugs bazaar – one of their logistics and financing centres – at Babaji in the Luy Manda Wadi just to the west of the Helmand.

They met with some resistance as they landed, but managed to consolidate while the remainder of the battlegroup in armoured vehicles, and ANSF, linked up with them for the push on Babaji. Despite the continual Taliban attacks, by 23 June the Scots had gained their objectives, though not without casualties. There were, however, far fewer civilian casualties than there might have been, since most had quit the area in the days and weeks before – indeed, in sudden numbers on the eve of the Scots' fly-in, as drone surveillance had reported. The implication was that they were forewarned of the assault: in other words, there'd been a breach of security, always a factor in operations with local forces of whatever nationality, and corrosive of trust.

Two days later, on 25 June, the Welsh Guards began advancing up the Shamalan canal, securing more crossing points to cut off Taliban lines of supply and thus prevent more fighters coming into the Babaji area. The Guards had taken casualties to IEDs even before their push began – on the first day of the operation, indeed – including a company commander killed. Then on 1 July the commanding officer himself, Lieutenant-Colonel Rupert Thorneloe, was killed accompanying a resupply column. News of these high-profile losses frayed yet more nerves in Westminster – Thorneloe had been the MA (military assistant) to Des Browne, the Secretary of State for Defence – as well as, in the words of one Light Dragoons SNCO, making everyone feel that bit more vulnerable and mortal.

Next day, the helicopter carrying the brigade commander ran into heavy fire and came close to being shot down. It was routine for helicopters to run into heavy fire, but again demonstrated that everyone was in it together. As expected, the Taliban were resisting hard. Mullah Omar had staked his and their reputation on dominance in Helmand that summer.

While the rest of the brigade were manning the cordon (the anvil), the Light Dragoons battlegroup were to be the hammer. The battlegroup was based on SHQ and two troops of A Squadron, all mounted in Jackals, two company groups of the Mercians, each with a troop of Scimitar, and the dismounted element of Emsdorf Troop.[12] Close-support sections from 125 Field Squadron RE were under command for breaching operations, and forward observation parties from 127 (Dragon) Battery RA. Battlegroup reserve was a Scimitar Troop (with Assaye Troop back under command in due course). In addition came two ANA companies with their mentoring teams, sixty Afghan police with their mentors, a troop of Viking carriers from

12. Emsdorf Troop's order of battle (orbat) for Panther's Claw: Lieutenant Rowley Gregg was to command the three Spartans (the troop-carrying – APC – variant of the Scimitar), and Lieutenant Charlie Dunn the three Scimitars. Sergeant Keith Bell was to command the dismounted fire support group (FSG) which consisted of a team of twelve including a sniper pair. The Scimitars' task was to act in intimate support of the platoons pushing forward, and Spartans' to provide armoured casualty evacuation and resupply. The FSG were to take up positions depending on the ground and situation. However, due to sustaining a significant number of casualties in the first two weeks, the orbat changed continually.

2RTR, plus two IED detection teams, search dogs and various other specialists. Meanwhile the Danish battlegroup with its troop of tanks and A Squadron left Camp Price outside Gereshk, heading south to clear Spin Masjed district, midway between Gereshk and Lashkar Gah, and to secure two further crossing points on the Nahr-e Bughra canal. The squadron detained some ninety fighting-age males crossing the river one evening.

The tanks were proof against the largest IEDs or mines – the most they could lose probably was a track – and their main armament, at 120 mm, could demolish a strongpoint at 2,000 metres. Their heavy machine guns too could bring down walls, but it was their menacing 'overwatch' – their observation and threat of fire while themselves invulnerable – that was their first strength. They'd no need of concealment – the Taliban had no weapon to deal with them – so could site themselves in a dominating position, traversing the turret as if minutely scanning the ground, which indeed they could with their advanced optics, and at night too, to reassure the ground troops and intimidate any would-be snipers. And in the event of IEDs and casualties, they could sprint to the scene with impunity and provide physical protection, something an Apache gunship, which could also menace, wasn't able to do. It remains another mystery why the Danes, who hadn't been at war since 1864, recognized the value of well-armed, well-armoured fighting vehicles – tanks – in Afghanistan, while the British, who'd only had one year (1968) since actually inventing the tank when they'd not lost a man in action, didn't.

While the boundaries of the battlefield were being secured, on 2 July the US marines, now with the same strategic intention as Panther's Claw, launched Operation Khanjar (Sword Strike) in the Helmand valley south of Lashkar Gah. In the absence of any real command from the two-star headquarters in Kandahar, it was an impressive piece of Anglo-American coordination by the respective brigade commanders and staff. The task force from the 2nd Marine Expeditionary Brigade and an ANA *kandak* swooped into the area by helicopter and armoured

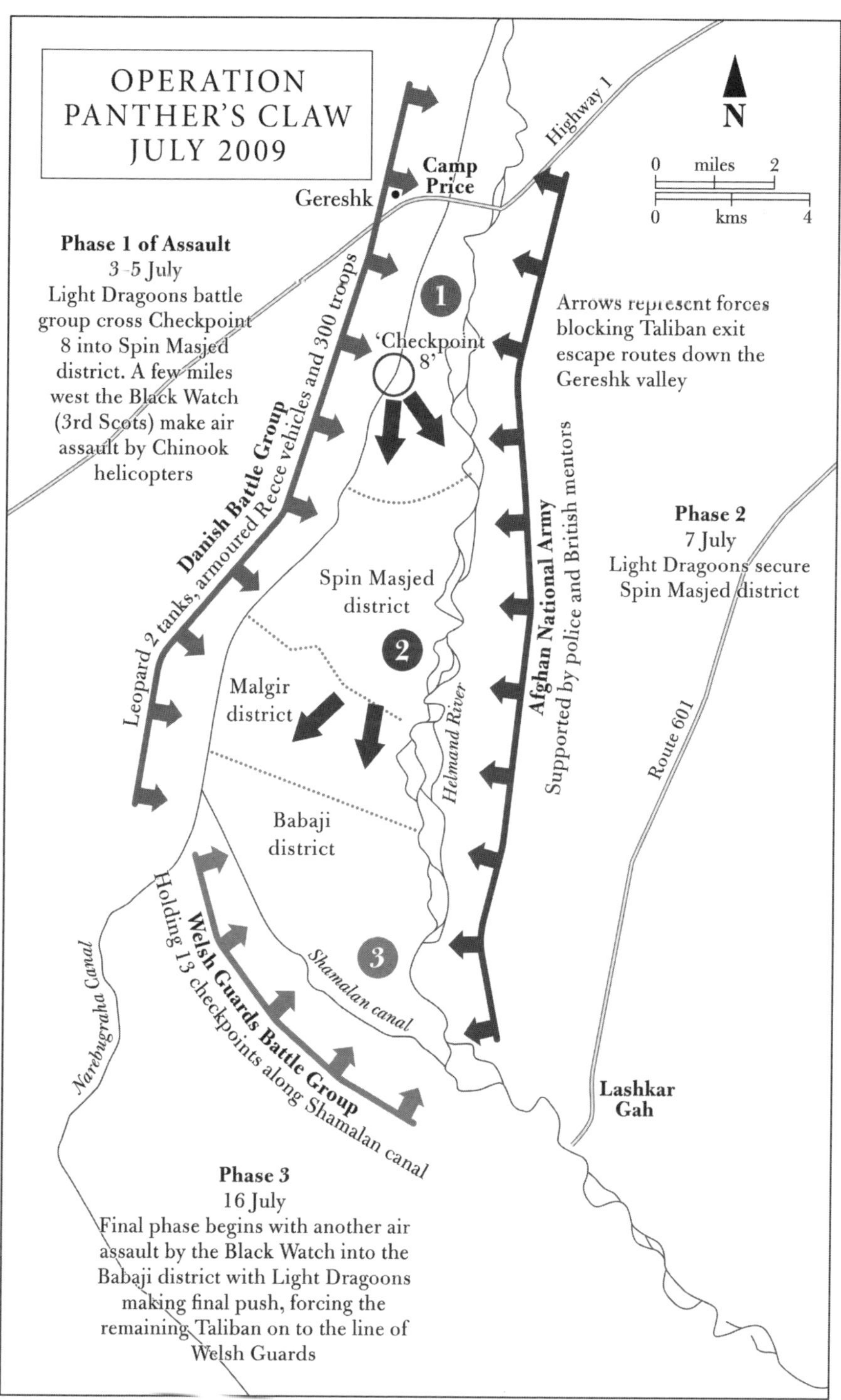
OPERATION
PANTHER'S CLAW
JULY 2009
Highway 1
N
0 miles 2
0 kms 4
Camp Price
Gereshk
Phase 1 of Assault
3–5 July
Light Dragoons battle group cross Checkpoint 8 into Spin Masjed district. A few miles west the Black Watch (3rd Scots) make air assault by Chinook helicopters
Danish Battle Group
Leopard 2 tanks, armoured Recce vehicles and 300 troops
'Checkpoint 8'
Arrows represent forces blocking Taliban exit escape routes down the Gereshk valley
Afghan National Army
Supported by police and British mentors
Phase 2
7 July
Light Dragoons secure Spin Masjed district
Spin Masjed district
Malgir district
Babaji district
Helmand River
Route 601
Shamalan canal
Narebugraha Canal
Welsh Guards Battle Group
Holding 13 checkpoints along Shamalan canal
Lashkar Gah
Phase 3
16 July
Final phase begins with another air assault by the Black Watch into the Babaji district with Light Dragoons making final push, forcing the remaining Taliban on to the line of Welsh Guards

vehicles, the biggest offensive airlift by the marines since the Vietnam War. Besides clearing the way for the August elections, Operation Khanjar would put paid to any large-scale Taliban counter-attack on the 19th Brigade.

The Panther's Claw battlefield had now been shaped. Or rather, the waterways that gave the Green Zone its shape were now secured (the Helmand river itself by ANSF and their British mentors), forming a massive cordon. Now the main phase could begin: a push by the Light Dragoons battlegroup from north-east to south-west between the Nahr-e Bughra canal and the Helmand to clear the entire area up to the Shamalan canal; in other words, to kill or capture the Taliban fighters, or to drive them on to the troops at the cordon – a drive of almost 10 miles.

It would prove tough going. Emsdorf Troop mounted element were attached to the Danish battle group for the initial breaking to the Spin Majid Wadi, and on 30 June moved down to FOB Price to join them. On 1 July they pushed forward with the Danes on a two-day operation into the wadi acting as fire support alongside three Leopard main battle tanks and a company of US special forces and ANA. The Danes conducted the break-in with the application of considerable 120mm fire from the Leopards, plus their 120 mortars, with the actual assault conducted by a mechanised company mounted in US-made M113 APCs.

The infantry's move across the wadi proved to be a slow process. Some two hundred IEDs had to be cleared from the wadi entrance alone. Once the Danes had broken in, Emsdorf Troop moved back to FOB Price late on 2 July and prepared overnight for the launch of the "hammer" phase of Panther's Claw next day.

At first light, the Light Dragoons battlegroup crossed the line of departure, A Company together with Emsdorf Troop (complete) conducting a "forward passage of lines" – always tricky, even without live ammunition – through the Danish battlegroup. Almost at once Lieutenant Dunn's Scimitar detonated an IED. The crew and the accompanying mine detection team were lifted off the ground but survived with relatively minor injuries. The Scimitar, however, was effectively destroyed. The Danish armoured repair and recovery vehicle, a variant of the Leopard, which came to recover it was disabled later that day by another IED. But A Company group rapidly regained momentum and cleared their objective over the next 24 hours without further significant incident.

On D+1 Lieutenant-Colonel Fair switched the battlegroup axis to B Company group, who now struck south over a canal crossing at the Abpashak Wadi to the east of A Company, using them as their western shoulder, followed by two ANA companies who provided eastern and rear flank security. Within the first 200 metres B Company was in small-arms contact. The initial contact was from the east, and following some "generous application of 30mm and coax", as Lieutenant-Colonel Fair put it, the fire-fight was emphatically won, and the ANA were launched to clear the Taliban firing position. Shortly afterwards an ANA soldier was killed in an IED blast and moments later an interpreter was killed in a second blast. As Lieutenant-Colonel Fair wrote in his summary of the operation, "This sadly set the tone for the following seven days."

During the seven days, indeed, the battle group would come across sixty-nine IEDs, a good many of which detonated before they were found. The direct fight was one thing, but this indirect fight – the war with the IED – would prove the more inhibiting, for the effect of an IED on an already methodical operation is almost always to slow it down further, even if the IED has first been detected. If it hasn't been detected, it can bring the operation to a standstill, for irrespective of the explosion's physical damage there is first the threat of a follow-up IED or a small-arms attack to deal with. Next are the casualties to treat and evacuate, and the consequences of the casualties to manage – the moral effect on the survivors, the loss of numbers and perhaps key capabilities, especially if the casualties include the tactical commander. In a conventional attack there is a naturally strong forward momentum, and casualties do not always slow the advance; but in a methodical operation such as Panther's Claw, dealing with ambush and casualties can easily *become* the operation itself.

Later that same day, 4 July, after continual contact in which the infantry and CVR(T) worked extraordinarily well together, an RPG hit one of Emsdorf's Spartans in a well-sited ambush by twenty or so Taliban. It detonated a box of grenades inside, killing Private Robert Laws of the Mercians, aged eighteen, and wounding four others. The Spartan's commander, Lieutenant Guy Disney, though badly wounded, managed to extricate his "waggon" from the ambush and report the contact by radio, adding: "I need a heli. I think I've lost my leg".[13] Others rushed to them over a bridge across an irrigation ditch, including Lieutenant-Colonel Fair. A casevac Chinook arrived quickly and the wounded were got away. A few minutes later, as one of Lieutenant-Colonel Fair's signallers, Lance-Corporal David "Duke" Dennis, crossed the bridge, an IED exploded beneath. Lance-Corporal Dennis died during the second casevac flight, which also took out others caught in the blast, including the Mercians' company commander and serjeant-major. Lieutenant-Colonel Fair ordered the company to withdraw 200 metres to a farm compound where they could reorganize and recover. The artillery FOO (Forward Observation Officer) assumed command and a Welsh Guards sergeant took over as CSM. Of the 2 kilometres that Lieutenant-Colonel Fair planned to clear that day, they'd managed only one.

Besides the constant IED threat, elusive fighters armed with, among other things, RPGs that were well able to destroy metal as well as flesh, would oppose the battlegroup for most of the way. The brigade post-operation report conceded that, contrary to the planning intelligence assessments, "[there] were a large number of INS [insurgents] determined and motivated to resist friendly forces advance. They had not buckled under the advance of two battle-groups, were not deterred

13. The leg was being held on by his radio operator, Lance-Corporal Kevin Turner. It would be amputated later, however. And yet he would return to the racing saddle, his great love, in remarkably quick time.

by the presence of armour, AH [attack helicopters] and aviation, and continued to fight despite heavy losses."

Indeed, said Brigadier Radford later, "The Light Dragoons were engaged in an extremely hard fight for five days ... an incredibly hard fight." After an overnight replenishment, with battle casualty replacements (BCRs) brought forward – including a new company commander, and the CQMS (company quartermaster-sergeant) taking over as CSM – the advance continued next morning. Lieutenant-Colonel Fair decided to change the advance from a one sub-unit up to a two-up formation, launching a company down the western flank, with his tactical headquarters (Tac HQ) between the two. Soon he had "the pleasure of hearing the company group win very convincingly in an almighty and lengthy contact on the eastern flank – much 30mm, 7.62, 5.56, bar mine and mortar to counter a not inconsiderable RPG- and PKM[14]-based engagement. B Company was back on its feet."

The bar mine, the army's Cold War period anti-tank mine, was used as a breaching-frame charge to blow holes in tough compound walls, thus avoiding the risk of triggering IEDs on established entry points and chokepoints within the compounds – especially IEDs with low metal content, and therefore almost undetectable.

B Company breached the final wall with their last few pounds of plastic explosive. Just short of the objective, however, Lance-Corporal Dane Elson of the Welsh Guards, commander of the fire-support team attached to the company, was killed instantly by an IED blast which wounded several others in – again – the company Tac HQ, including Sergeant Grant Cuthbertson LD, the tactical air controller (JTAC: Joint Terminal Attack Controller), who had only joined that night as a BCR.

The company had also begun to take heat casualties, many of which were subsequently identified as manifestations of varying degrees of battle shock. Company groups and BG Tac HQ overnighted in the

14. *Pulemyot Kalashnikova* – a Russian GPMG equivalent.

same compound in what Lieutenant-Colonel Fair described as "a very sombre atmosphere."

Within minutes of stepping off the next morning, A Company were in contact again. The dismounted element of Emsdorf Troop, acting now as the company fire support group, were caught in another RPG-initiated ambush. Four of the troop, including Sergeant Keith Bell, one of the dismounted section commanders, were casevac'd. While A Company pressed on, Lieutenant-Colonel Fair and his Tac HQ moved back to the western flank to join B Company, who soon began to take more heat casualties, and he decided therefore not to commit them for the rest of the day. A Company group, with its Scimitars, managed to clear much of the route that became a key interior line of communication for the battlegroup. At one point they were blowing several suspected IEDs within yards of each other. Besides the immediate challenge of where to place the next foot, however, the battlegroup was continuing its efforts in depth, using a combination of air, human and electronic surveillance methods to identify key leaders or groups. Once these were positively identified and "de-conflicted" from the local population, they were struck by indirect fire – in one engagement destroying a concentration of some forty Taliban.

The following day, 7 July, was something of a turning point. B Company group advanced at first light and made good progress in the relative cool of the morning. They had the initiative and pre-empted several Taliban contacts, killing many and generating some decisive momentum. Mercifully, they took no further battle casualties and were able to maintain the momentum through the remainder of the operation. A Company group, now with an ANA company following up, had more contacts, largely harassing engagements from the west which were generally resolved through 30mm or indirect fire and followed up by ANA, which allowed the Mercians to focus on the advance. However, in one of the latter compound clearances, an IED killed Trooper Christopher Whiteside of Emsdorf Troop, wounding two others from the troop and a sapper.

Then overnight a Viking detonated an IED, wounding three, and in a final contact on 9 July, as the two Mercian company groups linked up around the south of the objective, an ANA soldier and an interpreter were seriously wounded by an IED, the interpreter subsequently dying of wounds. Brigadier Radford now reinforced the battlegroup with a company of 2nd Rifles and a company of 3rd Scots (Black Watch). This, said Lieutenant-Colonel Fair, injected additional momentum and carried the battlegroup onto the second objective, which was taken without a shot fired: "Unlike the initial objective, this was still well populated and had very good atmospherics. The apparently genuine welcome we received was warming and particularly rewarding given the events of the previous week."

On 10 July a strong company group of the 3rd Scots was lifted by Chinook forward of the LD BG to confuse the Taliban; and the battlegroup began its final advance of three miles with renewed momentum. A Black Watch officer later recounted how his company had heard on the radio the "completely calm, almost nonchalant but clipped voice procedure" as they approached, and how it raised their morale. Lieutenant-Colonel Fair recalled how "watching these final Eastern Front-esque advances of multiples of men interspersed with CVR(T) moving with momentum as far as one can see across the fields and irrigation ditches was warming after the previous week of hard fighting."

The IEDs had undoubtedly taken their toll on momentum as well as on flesh throughout the brigade. It was the old story: "Objectives that were meant to have been overwhelmed in an hour took more than a day to seize," as the MoD's Media Ops (London) blog reported. "We were essentially manoeuvring in a giant minefield," added one of the Light Dragoons. And in temperatures of almost 40 degrees.

Anxiety had certainly been mounting in Downing Street. On 13 July, the prime minister, Gordon Brown, rang Brigadier Radford to ask if he had enough helicopters. Radford replied that he'd made his plans with what he'd got, and that although it was enough he could do with more helicopters and also more manpower to build on the results of the operation.[15] This was the first major offensive operation in the history of the British army in which heliborne forces played a sustained and integrated part. Without helicopters it would have taken an entirely different shape and course – if indeed it had been carried out at all.[16]

By 14 July the Light Dragoons battlegroup were nearing their final objective, a line from the Nahr-e Bughra canal south and east to the Helmand river, just before the river turns further south and the Green Zone widens. Brigadier Radford told the battlegroup to pause in Malgir area to recuperate and resupply, and to allow the Mercians and their ANA contingent to secure checkpoints and compounds in the cleared zone. From here, other elements of the brigade would take on the final push towards the Shamalan canal.

A week later, the brigade had cleared a further hundred compounds and the remaining seven miles of the Green Zone, but at continuing and increasingly high-profile cost. On 18 July, 26-year-old Captain

---

15. In parliament on 15 July, with casualties now a daily concern of the national media, the leader of the opposition, David Cameron, pressed the prime minister on the issue: "Is not the basic problem this: the number of helicopters in Afghanistan is simply insufficient? Will the Prime Minister confirm that the American marines, who have approximately the same number of troops as us in Helmand, are supported by some 100 helicopters, whereas our troops are supported by fewer than 30?" To which the PM replied that he'd spoken to Radford, who'd said "[he] has sufficient to get on with the task ... he's been given". This, of course, omitted the material point, that more helicopters were needed to do the job properly. Radford had also told the PM that he needed "more and better ANSF in order to lead to transition and more helicopters which would greatly enhance our tactical effectiveness" (Radford's diary). In choosing to represent the conversation with Radford in this way, ignoring its import, the PM laid himself open to accusations of disingenuousness, which persist. While tactical operations aren't a "no-go area" for policy, the manner of contact needs special care, not least to avoid misunderstanding by a policy-maker not familiar with tactical matters. The question ought to have been asked of the Chief of the Defence Staff, who would then have been obliged to answer fully, and held to account by parliament. And the CDS ought to have insisted on it.
16. The army and Royal Marines had, of course, had a good deal of experience in helicopter operations – in Malaya, Suez, Borneo, Northern Ireland and the Falklands – but Panther's Claw was a considerable gear change.

Harry Parker of The Rifles had been severely wounded, losing both legs. His father was Lieutenant-General Sir Nick Parker, the army's deputy C-in-C, who was about to take over as General McChrystal's second-in-command in Kabul. When the news was broken to him, he said it made him even more determined that they did the job properly.

The final phase to take key ground surrounding Babaji could now be launched: heliborne assaults by the 3rd Scots behind the Taliban to pin them in place, while the company-group from the 2nd Royal Welsh in sixty armoured vehicles, including the well-protected Warrior tracked armoured infantry fighting vehicle, pushed into the area from the south-east – all led by Assaye Troop. By 27 July Babaji itself was secured. Intelligence estimated that in all some 200–300 Taliban had been killed, out of perhaps some 500 active in the Green Zone (the actual body count was low, with the Taliban always trying to recover their dead), and resistance was clearly crumbling. Brigadier Radford called a halt. It was time for consolidation.

The IED danger was certainly not past, however. On 4 August, Lance-Corporal Anthony Lombardi, a REME vehicle mechanic (VM) attached to Emsdorf Troop was killed in the driving seat of a Spartan during a resupply convoy escort. Sergeant Gavin Harvey, the vehicle commander, lost both legs. A month later, another REME VM, Lance-Corporal Richard Brandon of A Squadron's fitter section, was killed instantly when the Samson CVR(T) recovery vehicle he was driving detonated an IED near Gereshk.

The purpose of Operation Panther's Claw being to allow the provincial elections to take place, rather than simply destroying the enemy, LD BG could now (after recovery, rest and replenishment at Camp Bastion) return to their TAOR to secure the polling stations against any resurgence of the Taliban. Polling day was not without incident, with many exchanges of fire, but voting went ahead.

During the final weeks on the ground, for A Squadron especially, Herrick 10 returned to the routine of patrolling, both mounted and dismounted. Concentrating its efforts on identifying areas of interest to the south for future brigade exploitation, the squadron ended its deployment with a particularly "crunchy" engagement while trying to work out the precise geographical limits of one particular village. Lucky to escape ambush, a fire-fight developed in which Trooper Aaron Deans was struck in the back by small-arms fire while at the wheel of his Jackal.

There was, in fact, no let-up until the battlegroup had handed over to the incoming Household Cavalry Regiment, and in November withdrawn to Camp Bastion for the return to barracks at Swanton Morley in Norfolk via a few days' "decompression" at RAF Akrotiri in Cyprus.

* * *

In his message to the regiment in the subsequent edition of the Journal, King Abdullah wrote: "As I followed your deeds from afar and saw the courage, skill, honour and fortitude with which you soldiered, I became ever more proud to be your colonel."

There was undoubtedly much courage and fortitude, but, as Churchill said, when it comes to honours and medals, "All that is possible is to give the greatest satisfaction to the greatest number and to hurt the feelings of the fewest. But that is a most difficult task and it is easy to err on one side or the other. One must be careful in the first place to avoid profusion. The tendency to expand, shall I say inflate, dilute the currency through generous motives, is very strong."

Not every act that inspired the colonel-in-chief's admiration could be recognized by an honour or award. Nevertheless, the number recognized in the operational awards list "for their services on Operation HERRICK 10" was impressive. In addition to Major Plant's MBE (Military), Lieutenant-Colonel Fair received a bar to his DSO for "inspirational leadership" (the original DSO awarded for Iraq while commanding a special forces squadron). Lieutenant Rowley Gregg, of Emsdorf Troop, was awarded the Military Cross for gallantry during Panther's Claw, the citation stating that: "Gregg insisted on leading from the front; resolute and firm in his determination to take the fight to the enemy at all costs. His courage, forthright leadership and determination to complete the mission in the face of heavy casualties were pivotal to the success of the operation. His bravery, leadership, and the outstanding personal example he set was exemplary." Five were mentioned in despatches "for gallantry during active operations": Sergeant Grant Cuthbertson, WO2 Mark Dobbs, Sergeant Jamie Lawson, Lance-Corporal Nigel Moffett (Killed in Action), Corporal Anthony Richardson. Corporal Leslie received the Queen's Commendation for Bravery (QCB), "for gallantry during active operations." Major Stuart Wiles received the QCVS for "meritorious service during, or in support of, operations". Three received the Joint Commander's Commendation for "commendable service during, or in support of, operations": Captain Tim Badham, Corporal Richard Hindson RAMC, and Lance-Corporal Gareth Beardshaw. A further eight received COMBRITFOR Commendations: Major Adam Bartholomew, Lieutenant Johnny Black, WO2 David Rae, Staff-Sergeant Barry Hall, Sergeant Terry Dove, Corporal Mark Evans, Trooper Matthew Littlewood (whose father was also serving in the regiment), and Trooper John Reid.

* * *

Perhaps the last word on The Light Dragoons during Herrick 10 should go to General McChrystal – an extract from his speech to The International Institute for Strategic Studies, London, in October 2009: "I am exceptionally proud to serve at ISAF. Within my office, I have a picture of a British battle group, led by Lieutenant Colonel Gus Fair, with whom I worked for a long time in Iraq. He is with his soldiers, who I had the opportunity to speak with when I visited them during operations in Spin Majid this summer in the Helmand River valley. I keep that picture because, when I looked into their eyes, which were bloodshot with fatigue, I remember the extraordinary professionalism, competence and the sheer courage of those young men. Whenever I come to London, I like to run through the city, and I particularly like the statues that you have directed to heroes. I hope that you erect one to that generation – they have earned it."[17]

* * *

Panther's Claw and what followed had considerable impact on the command arrangements in southern Afghanistan too. In May the following year ISAF decided that Regional Command (South) would be split into two new headquarters and areas of responsibility. The British government (the new Conservative-Liberal coalition following the defeat of Labour at the recent general election) announced it in these terms:

> *A new Regional Command (South West), based in Helmand, will oversee Helmand and Nimruz provinces; while the existing Regional Command (South), headquartered in Kandahar, will continue to control ISAF forces in Kandahar, Daykundi, Uruzgan and Zabul provinces.*
>
> *This change, which is based on the military advice of ISAF commanders on the ground, reflects a number of significant changes over recent months and was welcomed today by the Defence Secretary, Dr Liam Fox.*
>
> *The recent changes on the ground include a large increase in the number of ISAF troops in southern Afghanistan – up from 35,000 in October 2009 to over 50,000 by this summer [2010] – and a greater complexity in the conduct of operations, with major ongoing security efforts in Kandahar and central Helmand.*

17. General McChrystal was relieved of command in June 2010 after he and members of his staff made derisive comments about senior officials in President Obama's administration to a reporter from – of all things – *Rolling Stone* magazine.

The new command structure will also enable a better alignment with Afghan National Army units, with 205 Corps continuing to work with Regional Command (South) [RC(S)] and 215 Corps partnered with the new Regional Command (South West).

The decision to divide responsibility between the two headquarters will help provide the best focus of command support for ISAF forces across the region.

Secretary of State for Defence, Dr Liam Fox, said:

"I welcome these changes to the command and control of our forces in Afghanistan which are based on sound military rationale and are in the interests of the overall coalition strategy and mission. Through their sheer professionalism, bravery and sacrifice, British forces have made real progress in Helmand. They will continue to do so working alongside Afghan, American and other ISAF partners making up an international effort of more than 45 nations."

Major General Gordon Messenger, the Chief of the Defence Staff's Strategic Communications Officer, said:

"This command and control change makes complete sense and is welcome. The span and complexity of the command challenge in southern Afghanistan has increased enormously in recent months and these changes provide the best command support to the troops on the ground. The change will also align the ISAF military structure in the south with the structure of the Afghan National Army, enabling a greater partnering capacity between ISAF and Afghan forces.

"The UK has been closely involved in the preparations for this change and entirely agrees with its rationale. We are well accustomed to operating within a multinational coalition command structure and are entirely content that the best interests of the UK force will be maintained under the new arrangements."

Looking to the future, Regional Command (South West) will operate under a rotational command, agreed in principle to be shared between US and UK forces. The first commander will be Major General Richard Mills of the US Marine Corps (USMC).

As part of the new arrangements, command and control boundaries will change within Helmand province.

Following the split, Task Force Helmand (TFH) will come under the command of the US Marine Corps' 1st Marine Expeditionary Force (1 MEF), under Major General Mills. TFH will retain responsibility for central Helmand.

Major General Richard Mills, Commanding General of 1st Marine Expeditionary Force (Forward), said:

"Regional Command (South West) will ensure that ISAF and Afghan forces in Helmand and Nimruz provinces achieve the objectives of Operation MOSHTARAK, which are intended to assert the Government of the Islamic Republic of Afghanistan's presence in the region.

"Since taking command six weeks ago I have been hugely impressed by the momentum and achievements of RC(S) under General Carter.

"My predecessors in the 2nd Marine Expeditionary Brigade and the British troops of Task Force Helmand have distinguished themselves in the service of the Afghan people. Real progress is being made.

"This will be the first time that the USMC has led an ISAF Regional Command. The British officers in my coalition headquarters and Task Force Helmand bring invaluable experience and knowledge. We are partnered with ANSF [Afghan National Security Forces] at all levels and conducting joint operations throughout Helmand province.

"While tough fighting remains, I see evidence daily of progress that will bring about lasting stability across southern Afghanistan.

"This will be a significant year for the future of Afghanistan. Coalition forces, alongside our Afghan counterparts, will continue to support the Government of the Islamic Republic of Afghanistan as it delivers legitimate governance, improved security and lasting economic development."

Additionally, under the changes, the command of the 1,100-strong British Battle Group based in Sangin and Kajaki will transfer from

Task Force Helmand to the US-led Regimental Combat Team (North), which is taking on responsibility for the north of the province.

In common with the other changes to ISAF's command structures, this transfer of command will take effect on 1 June 2010 and is intended to optimise the command support available to the troops on the ground in light of the increased number of ISAF troops and other operational assets.

ISAF intends for Regional Command (South West) to become fully operational later this summer. In order to ease the transition, there will be an interim phase where 1 MEF will take responsibility for Helmand and Nimruz but will continue to work to Regional Command (South). This arrangement is planned to run from 1 June.

The UK-led Provincial Reconstruction Team in Helmand will work closely with the headquarters of Regional Command (South West) and will continue its vital role in delivering governance and socio-economic development in the province.

The announcement ended with a firm assurance: "UK forces are committed to their enduring deployment to central Helmand and there are no plans to deploy UK forces from Helmand to anywhere else."

There was still work to be done by The Light Dragoons in Helmand.

Chapter Six

Herrick 16: May to October 2012

"What's going to happen this spring is that Afghans will be in the lead throughout the country."

Arguments continue as to just how successful – or indeed necessary – Operation Panther's Claw was. When it ended, General McChrystal came down from Kabul and addressed the brigade. He said that President Obama had told him that he had to deliver success in a year: "What I needed was a victory, and this is it."

It was certainly a tactical success in driving out the Taliban, holding out hope that Lashkar Gah and Gereshk could be joined up, and making for continuity with the brigade that would replace the 19th in November. But voter turnout on 20 August proved low throughout southern Afghanistan, probably because of a remaining Taliban presence ample enough to intimidate and coerce the local population. After all, the operation had been expected and its strategic purpose well understood, and besides resisting the brigade's attempt to clear the area, the Taliban must have calculated on enough of them being able to lie low or re-infiltrate once the operation was ended. Brigadier Radford had always understood this: "How do we know you'll stay?" had been the question on the lips of every Afghan staking his future on the operation. One of his answers had been what he called "hot stabilization", the immediate follow-up by the PRTs to begin the development projects that the Taliban's presence had prevented. It was on a par with "courageous restraint". But holding cleared territory was meant to be the responsibility of the ANSF, with British support and mentors, and they proved not yet up to the task in either number, commitment or reliability. Indeed, their heart, and that of the Afghan civil authorities, wasn't yet in it. Nor, evidently, had been that of the commander of ISAF Regional Command (South), a Dutch major-general, who might have allocated more resources to the operation, including helicopters and explosive ordnance disposal, if he'd truly judged that it represented his command's main effort.

British officials, military and civilian (FCO, which of course had the notional lead), had stressed that Panther's Claw and continuing operations in the summer and autumn months would be crucial, not just in taking decisive military action against the Taliban but also to convince public opinion in Britain that the ANSF would be increasingly responsible for their country's security. The task for British and other alliance troops would then be to train these forces and develop a proper civil infrastructure. Panther's Claw showed, however, that there needed to be another reset – or at least considerable retuning – of the campaign.

It also showed that the British army was indeed prepared to shed blood. But the casualties had been more than expected – back in Britain, that is. Casualties are casualties, whatever the rank, but one or two were names that were known in Westminster, and touched a few more nerves than usual. They were also particularly harrowing, with reports of multiple amputees, and they continued after the operation was declared at an end. In fact, though, the casualties during Panther's Claw weren't significantly greater than the average during the brigade's six-month tour as a whole (seventy-six killed and 340 notifiable casualties, of which thirty were amputees). But they caused great political difficulties for the prime minister, Gordon Brown, for now the unpopularity of the Iraq War, which was seen as "Blair's war", its opprobrium accordingly attaching not to him but to his predecessor, had attached itself to the Afghan War. And the same unforced errors of the Iraq War, notably the slow fielding of adequately protected vehicles and second-rate care and support for wounded troops on return – and their families – were remorselessly censured by the media and opposition parties. Helicopters were the totemic issue. By now it was clear to all but the purblind that there weren't enough, and never had been enough; and the government's attempts to persuade people otherwise made matters even worse, for there was now to all intents and purposes a breakdown in civilian–military trust. And Gordon Brown could expect no quarter, for as chancellor of the exchequer during the first ten years of Labour government from 1997 he'd insisted on defence cuts that had led to those very reductions in capability. Although, that said, a lack of inter-service spending coherence and botched procurement certainly hadn't helped.

British military policy in Afghanistan – or, perhaps better put, the focus of the campaign's strategy – now changed very decidedly. The emphasis switched almost exclusively to training the ANSF and getting them to take the lead, with October 2014 set as the date for withdrawal of all combat forces – "tough love." Thereafter, just a few hundred trainers and advisors would remain, the minimum to honour the continuity promised to the Afghans. (Sceptics – cynics perhaps – had argued for some time that the "exit strategy" for Afghanistan should be to declare victory then quit.) In November 2009, the British Major-General Nick Carter took over Regional Command (South). This was a significant move. General Carter's operational experience was huge, and he was both willing and able to take command of what in effect was a division, rather than leaving matters for subordinate commanders to arrange among themselves.

General McChrystal gave him command of Operation Moshtarak, to be launched in February to clear the Taliban from Marjah district, a major stronghold. Moshtarak – "Together", significantly, in Dari, Afghanistan's lingua franca – involved two simultaneous offensives, one by a US Marines task force in Marjah south of Nad-e Ali, and one by TFH in the north of Nad-e Ali. Both Generals McChrystal and Carter were determined that Moshtarak would be a politically led effort in full partnership with ANSF – hence the name. Crucially, and in contrast with Panther's Claw, the Afghan government pledged to hold any territory seized during the assault with Afghan forces, which meant both raising more of them and diverting existing forces to Helmand from elsewhere, notably Kabul and the east. In turn, even greater emphasis on "courageous restraint" would enhance legitimacy. It was no coincidence that on Moshtarak the use of high-explosive artillery shells went down by more than 60 per cent, while the use of smoke shells to mask movement went up by nearly 70 per cent. Critically, though, General Carter, who nine years later would become Chief of the Defence Staff, also took great pains to secure, as it were, his home flank – UK public opinion.[1] He wanted Moshtarak to end when it had achieved its strategic object, rather than when nerves frayed in Whitehall. In that respect, too, Panther's Claw had shaped Moshtarak, both directly in terms of tactical lessons learned, and indirectly by its impact at home.

Battles always have strategic consequences, because operational strategy is the employment of the battle as the means of attaining the object in war – the object being the first element of policy. And policy, while not precisely the same as politics, is ultimately political. Policy shapes battles by design. Battles shape politics often as not by chance.

By 2009, then, there had been broad agreement that the war should be brought to an end, but *how* was the major issue for the 2009 presidential elections that re-elected Hamid Karzai.[2] He called on "our Taliban brothers to come home and embrace their land" – peacefully, he meant – and began plans for another loya jirga. His efforts, arguably, were undermined by President Obama's massive troop increase, and at the London conference in January 2010 he repeated that he wanted to reach out to the Taliban. Hillary Clinton, US Secretary of State, gave him cautious support, and the so-called "Peace Jirga" was held in

1. The Light Dragoons were fortunate throughout their six years of deployments in enjoying strong public support in their recruiting areas and also in Norfolk, especially the town of Dereham, close to Robertson Barracks at Swanton Morley.
2. In 2009 Brigadier Simon Levey (LD) became commander of the British Combined Arms Training Group tasked with training the ANA.

Kabul the following June, attended by some 1,600 delegates. But the Taliban did not attend.

President Karzai confirmed in June 2011 that secret talks were taking place between the US and the Taliban, but by August 2011 these had collapsed, and further attempts in 2012 and 2013 stalled over both substantial as well as presentational issues, not least, as Karzai complained, the Taliban portraying themselves as a government in exile.

On 2 May 2011, however, there was what appeared to be a major strategic success for the Alliance: al-Qaeda's "First General Emir", Osama bin Laden, was killed by US special forces, and the fact that his hideaway was in Pakistan triggered intense international interest. The Pakistani government denied that it had sheltered bin Laden, saying it had been sharing information with the CIA and other intelligence agencies about him since 2009. However, it was clear that there would be something of a sea change in cooperation, with Pakistan upping its game so to speak, so that in June President Obama felt able to announce that 10,000 troops would be withdrawn from Afghanistan by the end of 2011 and an additional 23,000 troops by the summer of 2012, leaving a little over 50,000. Canada at once withdrew its combat troops, announcing that it would remain in a training role only. Other NATO and Alliance countries announced troop reductions. However, in the months after bin Laden's death, Taliban attacks continued at the same intensity as before, if not greater.

President Karzai would visit the US in January 2012. During the visit he and President Obama agreed to transfer combat operations from Nato to Afghan forces by spring the following year. "What's going to happen this spring is that Afghans will be in the lead throughout the country", said Obama afterwards. "They [ISAF forces] will still be fighting alongside Afghan troops… [but] we will be in a training, assisting, advising role", adding that "We achieved our central goal, or have come very close… which is to de-capacitate al-Qaeda, to dismantle them, to make sure that they can't attack us again" and that any US mission beyond 2014 would focus solely on counter-terrorism operations and training.

President Richard Nixon had adopted the same approach to Vietnam in 1969, which became known as "Vietnamization." In his national security decision memorandum he stated "There will be no de-escalation [withdrawal of support to the process] except as an outgrowth of mutual troop withdrawal." However, he also directed the development of a "Specific plan timetable for Vietnamizing the war," or withdrawing US troops and shifting the burden to the South Vietnamese to carry on the war, and squaring this circle by claiming that withdrawing US forces was not "de-escalation" as long as South Vietnamese forces replaced departing US forces — which was of course exposed as wishful thinking by the South Vietnamese Army's subsequent performance. The Vietnamization experience might reasonably have been taken as a salutary lesson by both politicians and soldiers. ("Study history, study history, in history lies all the secrets of Statecraft"). It was not. Or rather, if it was at all, it was taken with a shrug. One British officer asking a senior commander if the handover to Afghan forces was "conditions based" received the reply, "Yes, and the condition is 'Time'."

NATO-member countries endorsed the exit strategy during the NATO Summit in May 2012. ISAF forces would transfer command of all combat missions to Afghan forces by the middle of 2013, and most of the 130,000 ISAF troops would leave by the end of 2014, when a new NATO mission would then assume a support role. It was into this strategic policy – or emerging policy – that The Light Dragoons deployed to Helmand for the last time: with 12 Mechanized Brigade again, Herrick 16, May to October 2012.

In his introduction to the 2012 Journal, Lieutenant-Colonel Sam Plant, who had commanded C Squadron during Herrick 10, wrote presciently of the coming tour: "We will deploy to Helmand at an exceptionally exciting and important time. Transition of security responsibility to the Afghan National Security Forces is of central importance to the UK's timely cessation of combat operations in

Afghanistan and over the course of our deployment this business of transition will really start to bite. Concurrently, we will continue to disrupt the Insurgency. This balance of mentoring and kinetic activity will test our powers of agility and flexibility to the maximum as we continually seek to adopt the most appropriate posture for any given situation."

The tasks the regiment faced required a degree of "disaggregation" even greater than on Herrick 10. RHQ was to form the core of the ISTAR Group HQ, within HQ 12 Mechanized Brigade, responsible for the command and control of nine sub-units totalling over 1,200 troops. Both A and B Squadrons were to deploy in recce roles: in broad terms, A Squadron would supply the tracked (CVR(T)) FR function, and B Squadron in the wheeled Jackal and dismounted role would compose the BRF. "The notion of independence of command and action at sub-unit level with brigade reconnaissance is very much alive and well", added Lieutenant-Colonel Plant. A significant proportion of D (Command & Support) Squadron was to work alongside the Welsh Guards in the Police Mentoring Advisory Group, and elements of HQ Squadron were to form the core of the brigade troops' echelon (ie the minor units not under command of one of the major units) in Camp Bastion. C Squadron with the remainder of HQ Squadron would have the critical role of "Rear Support Squadron" in Swanton Morley. In former times, the function of keeping the home fires burning while the rest were away fell to an ad hoc rear party usually based on the assistant adjutant, the families officer, and the regimental band – the latter by this time long gone. The term "rear support", however, properly reflected the considerable physical and moral support required for each deployment.

Lieutenant-Colonel Plant concluded by saying that "The Regiment is well trained and prepared and I look forward to providing details of yet more LD success on operations in next year's Journal."

The essence of the tour was dispersal and continual reorganization, not surprising in an operation in support of the ANA – whose training and mentoring needs were, to say the least, "emerging" – while at the same time having to keep a lid on the insurgency, if only from the force protection point of view. By the end of April, A Squadron under Major Ollie King were in MOB Price in Nahri Saraj District (alternatively called Gereshk District), taking over as the FR squadron from the Queen's Dragoon Guards. Although TFH (brigade) troops, they would in fact be working primarily to the ISTAR group headed by RHQ at Lashkar Gah. The role of FR had changed considerably since they were there in 2009, and noticeably more than previous tours in 2006/7. The squadron began operations with three sabre troops in Scimitars (much upgraded and up-armoured), a support troop in Spartans, and an FSG troop in Jackals, with SHQ in Jackals or Huskies and an attached fire-support team (FST) in Coyotes.[3] No sooner had they got into the swing of operations, however, than 2nd, 4th (Support) and 5th (Guided Weapons, but in a "generalist" role) troops were re-roled as Afghan police advisors and attached to various units of the brigade. This change in orbat left the squadron looking markedly thinner, but still with the two sabre troops commanded by Captains Will Tod and Freddie Paske, with Sergeants Steve Sampher and Matty Newell. SHQ still had the FST as an asset and was periodically allocated elements of the brigade "Ops Company" in tracked Warthog APCs (similar to Viking), which would prove to be more than enough firepower, manoeuvre and search capability for all FR operations.

The main areas of operations were to the north of the task force area, in the Upper Gereshk Valley under control of the 2nd Royal Welsh battlegroup. Sergeant Sampher and his crew soon proved the integrity of the Scimitar with its rollover protection system in an IED strike, all surviving with relatively minor injuries. Indeed he and his crew were blown up twice during the tour, each time the vehicle being

3. The Husky is a four-man 4x4-drive enclosed, protected "pickup" type vehicle with a machine gun on the roof. The Coyote is a 6×6 tactical support vehicle (TSV), a "stretched Jackal" by Supacat, with a payload for supplies and equipment of 1.5 tons, and armed with a .50 calibre MG or a 40mm Grenade MG in addition to the GPMG.

completely destroyed. Sergeant Sampher proved the integrity of the crew helmet during this ambush, a sniper round partially penetrating. The squadron also briefly held the record for the largest home-made explosives find of the summer, under a tarpaulin in a wadi. Halfway through the tour Major King handed over command to Major Will Leek of the Scots Dragoon Guards, while Captains Tod and Paske left for postings to the Army Foundation College in Harrogate, with Lieutenants Ed Glover and Will McManners replacing them. Change was quite evidently in the air at every level.

August brought increased activity, with the squadron working for the Grenadier Guards to the north of Gereshk, and again for King's Royal Hussars battlegroup in a number of major operations to clear and hold the insurgent stronghold of Pupulzai, in conjunction with US Army engineers' route-proving and clearance teams with ground-penetrating radar and mine rollers to survey safe routes. In September the main effort switched to the south and centre of the task force TAOR as part of the brigade's wider main effort, until in October the emphasis switched again to handover to the incoming unit, the Queen's Royal Lancers.

But on 9 September the squadron suffered a bitter blow, when Sergeant Lee Davidson, with one of the police advisory teams (PATs), was killed in the north west of Nahr-e Saraj district when his Ridgback detonated a huge IED.[4] His future in the Light Dragoons, said Lieutenant-Colonel Plant, "was full of promise, and continued promotion up the ranks was a given." Trooper "Johnny" English sustained a serious back injury, and Corporal "Abba" Fernandez would later have a leg amputated due to blast injuries. Trooper "Acko" Atkinson was also shot in the buttock by a sniper.

B Squadron, with its attached electronic warfare team and FST, having begun arriving in theatre in mid-March, assumed responsibility

4. Ridgback: an up-armoured version of the Cougar MRAP (Mine Resistant Ambush Protected) vehicle, a 4×4 produced by Force Protection Industries Incorporated of South Carolina, who had also developed the Mastiff.

for the BRF in the second week of April. They were at continuous short (60 minutes) notice-to-move for operations, but of course always at instant readiness for emergencies – if "come as you are". Such a regime places an enormous strain on maintenance and logistics, and a premium on crew rest, but, at least at the beginning of the tour, emergencies were fewer, for the Afghan farmers were well underway with their main poppy harvest, a labour-intensive process that had a significant effect in the reduction of the insurgents' willingness to initiate hostilities, if not their hostile intent.

Two days into the first week of operational responsibility, however, the squadron was given its first short-notice, time-sensitive operation, the warning order received mid-afternoon and the objective in Hyderabad, Upper Eastern Gereshk Valley, an area ominously nicknamed "The Heart of Darkness." With dusk approaching and the troops resting following a helicopter assault the previous day, the call to muster went out. While the command team pored over maps and studied the live footage from a drone, the troop sergeants corralled some ninety troops into their three pre-designated chalks for insertion by Chinook. Within thirty minutes of receiving the warning order, the chalks were complete and the confirmatory kit-checks had begun. Within ninety minutes, troop orders had been delivered, maps printed and distributed and the green light given. Three Chinooks, rotors turning, were waiting as the squadron arrived at the flight line, which they found an impressive sight after being used to seeing just the one during pre-deployment training.

The objective was a suspected cache of explosives in a compound, and it was expected that there would be IEDs laid defensively. On landing, therefore, the search-dogs were sent forward of the point men, which would prove to be the start of a close bond between the troops and one dog in particular, which during the search of the compound by 3rd Troop located five IEDs. None of the IEDs had been activated, however, due to the tactical surprise and speed with which the troops had been able to advance from the landing site (LS), thanks in considerable part to attack-helicopters circling overhead and 1st and 2nd Troops providing flank protection. Indeed, the Taliban had left everything in their rush to escape (the chai they were drinking was still warm in the pot): 250kgs of explosive, 64 pressure-plates and other items of bomb-making equipment, most of which was destroyed in place and the rest brought back to Camp Bastion for closer examination. 3rd Troop made a pyre of home-made explosives, IEDs, pressure plates, ammunition, bags of raw opium, and, just so the Taliban couldn't run away so quickly next time, threw on their motorbikes as well as the shoes they'd left behind in a rush.

Within ninety minutes of first landing, the Chinooks returned to the LS, where the squadron had rallied for "exfiltration", at which point the Taliban opened fire. The Apaches returned fire, and the exfiltration went off without a hitch. It was only back at Camp Bastion that the bullet holes in the Chinooks' fuselages were discovered.

The operational tempo continued high. The first squadron ground-assault operation took place towards the end of April in the Arghandab River valley to the south of the TF TAOR, which the Taliban were suspected of using as a transit route. The ISTAR group (the EWT, FST and 2nd Troop) and SHQ took up over-watch at first light, with 1st and 2nd Troops screening the flanks, while 3rd Troop was dropped off by Warthogs to probe into the cultivated area. Heavy machine gun fire forced 1st Troop to break contact and withdraw, and 3rd Troop were engaged with small-arms fire and RPGs throughout the morning as they cleared west. An AK47 round penetrated the electronic IED-counter-measures pack on Lance-Corporal "Jackie" Milburn's back, and Lieutenant Ian Massey in his Jackal was hit by a .5inch armour-piercing round, though both were treated just for minor injuries. Then as the ISTAR group were re-positioning on the high ground, SSM Carl Loughney's vehicle, the last in the line, detonated an IED, which resulted in his three crew members being casevac'd, which he himself coordinated, although badly knocked about.

A few days later the squadron took part in a helicopter assault to block the Taliban in the Upper Gereshk Valley in support of an operation by the Grenadier battlegroup. There were a lot of Taliban in the area and the Warthogs had already taken two hits from IEDs when 1st Troop returned to search a suspicious structure they'd noted earlier in the day. They came under heavy and accurate small arms and RPG fire almost at once, but fought through to the objective, where they discovered more explosives and bomb-making equipment. Once this had been destroyed, neutralized, or collected for exploitation, they began making their way back, but an IED was detonated. Trooper Cayle Royce was very seriously injured, and was only saved by the skill of Corporal Ian Jackson RAMC, the troop medic, and the quick thinking of Sergeant James Short and others round him – as well as Trooper Royce's own considerable strength and fitness. Indeed, although he would lose both legs above the knee and several fingers of his left hand, less than two years later Cayle Royce and a fellow amputee would row the Atlantic to raise money for the Limbless Ex-Servicemen's Association.

Meanwhile, D Squadron's Herrick was nothing if not variegated. The mission was to staff the Lashkar Gah training centre, man the district advisory team (DAT) in Nar e Saraj, support the Police Mentoring Advisory Group (PMAG) HQ, and also the mentoring of the Afghan National Civil Order Police (an ANA force with the imaginative abbreviation ANCOP) whose mission was to provide deterrence-reassurance patrols, prevent violent public incidents, and provide crisis and anti-terror response in urban areas, especially Kabul and the provincial capitals. The DAT in Nar e Saraj was due to take sixty Danish soldiers under command and, while Captain Will Carver went to support their training in Denmark, the squadron leader, Major Charlie Colbeck, went to Helmand to observe the Police Operational Mentoring and Liaison Team (POMLT). Subsequently he would write, "it was clear that they [the Afghan police] were at the forefront of the counter-insurgency fight and we started to understand why some classic policing might have been overlooked."

The experience of the Nar e Saraj advisory team is illustrative. The team consisted of seven Light Dragoons and deployed so early that they were serving under 20th Armoured Brigade (Herrick 15) for a good while. The initial shock was the diversity of capbadges in such a small space, including the sixty Danes, whose capbadges were equally diverse, and six Danish civilian policemen to provide expert advice to the mentors. The initial impression was of a tight-knit but functioning military organization in a city that had been quiet over the previous months, notwithstanding frequent change of district chief of police. The situation was, however, to change dramatically.

Major Colbeck pondered on the enigma that was Gereshk, well-known as a busy hub for all sorts of trade and activity:

> "Many wise men, some at great length, have tried to articulate the reason that in the midst of turmoil down the centuries it seems to have carried on almost oblivious to the conflicts, and why this equilibrium should remain. The almost unanimous conclusion is: 'It's complicated'. The Danish T-shirt at the end of the tour captured it perfectly: 'If it makes sense, it isn't Gereshk'. They had summed up rather neatly the complicated and equally intriguing city that gave us the backdrop for a fascinating tour and one that provided a huge number of challenges that not even the latest version of MST [mission-specific training] could have prepared us for. Following the handover period, the situation in the city quickly deteriorated to what could be politely described as chaotic and suddenly we were at the epicentre of a time of great change and uncertainty; the oddest result was that we were hosting a large number of high profile visits!"

It didn't help when during the transitional period the provincial chief of police suddenly replaced almost a hundred policemen across the district, leaving the advisory team as a whole with almost no corporate knowledge, and the team from the Princess of Wales's Royal Regiment (from whom the LD team were taking over) rather disconsolate as they visited their checkpoints to find all the personnel had changed, and with it the sense that their entire tour had been for naught.

Attacks on the police suddenly increased – IEDs and checkpoint shootings, though it was not always clear who was behind the attacks, as the Taliban did not always claim responsibility. In this new "climate of extreme hostility", said Major Colbeck, it was clear that "we had to innovate, coming up with a strategy that would have to aim for some reachable targets (simpler logistics, command empowered to a lower level, intelligence-led policing and an acceptance of training for its benefits) and have to take into consideration the changed circumstances and the nature of the uniformed police in Nar e Saraj. The advisory team broke down into areas that required various levels of support and mentoring, on the surface seemingly pretty sensible breaking-down into the functional areas familiar to the military."

Personnel and logistics became the focus for Sergeant James Price, who "due to some very hard work and perseverance [in the face of downright corruption] managed to effect change in the way that logistics were handled across Nar e Saraj." Intelligence was handled by Staff-Sergeant Paul Grahame and Corporal Matthew Purvis, who formed good relationships with the officers on the ground, again to circumvent the corruption in the district headquarters. Operations were mentored by the squadron leader and the Danish second in command (a captain). Watch-keeping was split across the team, with the daytime duty falling to Sergeant Leslie Moon and Corporal Ashley Cheetham, both of whom also acted as a foreman of signals (the post of equipment manager in the Royal Corps of Signals), especially for electronic counter-measures.

One of their most significant contributions was to arrange complete radio coverage across the city for the PATs, something hitherto ignored, which greatly boosted confidence in the ability to support those on the ground – for the most part the Welsh Guards and the Danish police liaison team, the latter who, in the words of the squadron leader, spoke terrifyingly good English.

In short, by this breaking-down into functional areas, the regiment's men proved to be substantial force multipliers.

"Overall it is hard to measure the effectiveness of mentoring on a universally accepted scale," wrote Major Colbeck afterwards. However, the trust gained by the mentors apparently generated a different approach to the policing of Gereshk from that found on arrival: "It is worth noting that the overriding issue that faced the Afghan police in February was allegations of corruption by the local population. These had faded to nothing by the end of April and from then on there was no further reporting of corruption by the locals. The police were no angels, but they had the support of the people that had been lacking in the past. D Squadron was spread thin for the tour, but punched above its weight."

This much could indeed be said for the regiment as a whole – just some 250 Light Dragoon cap-badged men – and was something of a test-bed for the role of "light cavalry" and "recce strike" being developed in theory in the MoD and Bovington. It was not a revolution, but an evolution, a natural development of armoured reconnaissance work in the Cold War, Bosnia and Iraq, accelerated by technology, necessity (numbers), and senior commanders' increasing familiarity with, and therefore trust in, recce troops.

"Although Helmand is not secure as we in the United Kingdom would recognise it, the centres of the major cities are more secure than when we arrived," concluded Captain Nick Durrans in the Journal the following year. "More schools are open than when we arrived. Prosecution of criminals and insurgents is more just than when we arrived. Most importantly the Regiment has contributed in no small part in transferring the responsibility and lead for security in Helmand Province from Nato to the Afghans and they have embraced it. For these reasons alone the Regiment stands proud."

The sentiment was echoed by the commanding officer in his introduction to the Journal, having said in the 2012 edition that he looked forward to providing details of yet more Light Dragoon success on operations: "The campaign in Afghanistan draws rapidly to a close and on Op HERRICK 16 we witnessed further significant steps forward. Since Op HERRICK 10, the Afghan National Army has transformed and witnessing their professionalism and determination was something to behold. They are now in the driving seat; ISAF is very much supporting."

He added, however, that while the regiment's contribution to Afghanistan was now over, "through Op HERRICKs 5, 6, 10 and 16 it is certain that we have made a real difference", but also that the contribution had come at significant cost: "We will always remember those who have paid the ultimate price and those who have sustained injuries."

* * *

By way of a coda to Herrick 16, which ended so full of hope and promise, as Remembrance Day approached soon after the regiment returned to Swanton Morley, Lieutenant-Colonel Sam Plant was interviewed (by the author) for *The Times*. The article – "The 'Northern Cavalry' in Afghanistan" – in which he reflects on the loss for the seeming gain, is reproduced below:

> On the Cenotaph — literally "empty tomb" — in Whitehall are inscribed the words, simply, "The Glorious Dead". The theological concept of Glorification, the full realisation of salvation, might be problematic to modern ears, even perhaps hollow-sounding to a soldier. General George S. Patton famously told his men "There's no glory in dying for your country, only in making the other SOB die for his." But the "magnificence" with which those killed in action in Afghanistan are repatriated touches the spirit deeply, says one recently returned commanding officer.
>
> Lieutenant-Colonel Sam Plant of The Light Dragoons is just back from Afghanistan, sitting with a cup of coffee in the kitchen

of our house in the middle of Salisbury Plain, as he had in March before the regiment was deployed to Helmand for six months with 12 Mechanized Brigade. He has the air of a man who knows his soldiers have done everything asked of them, and more, but not without a price. Besides the injuries treated in-theatre, one of his dragoons, Trooper Cayle Royce, is now at Headley Court, the forces' rehabilitation centre, battling back with two prosthetic legs. And one of his oldest regimental comrades, Sergeant Lee Davidson, was killed by a Taliban mine, leaving a wife, two young sons and a third child due in a few weeks' time.

"The absolute dignity and respect in dealing with casualties, both fatal and non-fatal is a vital ingredient of morale in Helmand," says Colonel Plant, who is full of praise for the medical and moral support at Camp Bastion and at the Queen Elizabeth Military Hospital at Selly Oak.

But if his dragoons have done their best, will it be good enough? Earlier I had attended a debriefing by the commander of 12 Mechanized Brigade, Brigadier Doug Chalmers, as I have with every one of the returning brigades since 2007. Chalmers, an understated infantryman, for whom Op Herrrick 16 has been the fourth tour of duty in Helmand, is modest in his claims. "I am a facilitator," he says: it is all about the gradual handover of the counter-insurgency campaign to the Afghan National Army (ANA) and police. He reveals that on Herrrick 16 the ANA destroyed more Taliban IEDs than did his own teams.

Not that this means that 12 Mechanized Brigade were merely trainers and mentors: The Light Dragoons alone located and removed, with ANA help, over three tonnes of Taliban explosives. But the action is increasingly at a distance from the centres of population: "The geography of the violence has changed," says Chalmers, the Taliban forced by security forces and civilians themselves into the barren lands.

This in turn has proved fruitful for Colonel Plant's dragoons in their role as reconnaissance troops, "operating beyond the fingertips of the ground-holders", where the combination of sophisticated surveillance equipment and old-fashioned scouting skills has kept up the attrition of the Taliban.

Not even the attempts to get to the nerve-ends of morale by the "green on blue" attacks — the killing of ISAF soldiers by men in ANA uniforms — are having appreciable strategic effect. "These are the hardest casualties to bear," says Colonel Plant, "but it's one of many risks, and not the most significant, though tiring having to keep your guard up."

It is far from over yet. Continuity remains high on the agenda. Colonel Plant has yet to go on leave, being instead on a round of "mission exploitation". "I am already talking to the commanding officer of the Household Cavalry, who will deploy to Helmand next spring," he tells me. "When we deployed in April the dragoons had such confidence in their training there was no loss of operational tempo on handover by the outgoing brigade."

This campaign maturity, not seen since Northern Ireland, is a real measure of professionalism.

But what next for the regiment? There are no plans for them to return to Afghanistan after this last, their fourth, tour. Instead they, like most regiments, are about to embark on "Transformation", the process of change from an Afghan-centric focus to one that is versatile enough to meet future contingencies under the plans known as "Future Force 2020". It will mean a new role for the regiment, as "light cavalry"; or rather, a consolidation of the role they have found themselves in on operations these past years — a move away from tracked armoured reconnaissance to wheeled scout cars and dismounted patrolling.

Colonel Plant has another year in command, and says his priority is to keep things together in what may seem something of a trough after 20 years of operations, for since its formation in 1992 by the amalgamation of the 13th/18th and the 15th/19th Hussars, The Light Dragoons have been almost permanently on an operational footing — first in the Balkans, then Iraq and Afghanistan. When their colonel-in-chief, King Abdullah of Jordan, a former officer in the regiment, visits next month it will be to present campaign medals to seasoned veterans.

His saddest task, however, may be to begin the reduction in the regiment's strength by up to a hundred dragoons. But Colonel Plant remains confident that they will still be able to recruit strongly in the regimental area — Yorkshire and the North-East — and have the pick of Sandhurst too: "I don't think our operational reputation could be higher, and that is everything."

This weekend, however, at its base in Norfolk, the regiment will be remembering the dead who have helped earn that reputation, while looking to support the families of those killed and injured in two decades of operations.

Colonel Plant himself will be presenting the Elizabeth Cross to Mrs Lee Davidson.

* * *

Again, there were honours for the battlegroup. The Military Cross was awarded "for exemplary gallantry during active operations on land" to Lance Corporal Stephen Shaw (RAMC). The Meritorious Service Medal "in recognition of good, faithful, valuable and meritorious service of those who are of irreproachable character and conduct" was awarded to WO1 (RSM) David Rae, and WO1 (ASM) Simon Sykes, REME. Joint Commander's Commendations were awarded to Lieutenant Colonel Plant, Lieutenant Edward Whitten, Sergeant Mark Allen, Sergeant Barry Taaffe, Sergeant James Short, Corporal Ian Dixon, and Corporal (Acting Sergeant) James Price.

LYNNE R. MOORE
2012

Postscript

From Op Herrick to Op Toral, and Finally Op Pitting

"The odds are on the cheaper man."

In December 2012, the prime minister, David Cameron, announced that 3,800 troops – almost half the tri-service force in Helmand – would be withdrawn during the following year, leaving some 5,200 personnel. And as planned, the UK ceased all combat operations in October 2014, and Herrick 20 (June – December) became the last roulement deployment under that name. From then, British military operations in Afghanistan were conducted under the codename Operation Toral, which was itself a sub-set of the Nato Operation Resolute Support (strictly, not an operation but a "Mission"). The word "Toral", like the other codenames, was randomly generated, with no obvious connection with Afghanistan. It is a female name of Indian origin meaning "folk heroine", and in geometry is the adjective of "torus", a surface formed by rotating a circle about a line that lies in the same plane but does not intersect it (e.g. like a ring doughnut). Either way, there may have been more to the connection than supposed, if only accidentally.

Toral had two major objects: training and mentoring Afghan forces, and providing protection for Nato advisors via the Kabul Security Force/ Kabul Protection Unit. Meanwhile, ANSF continued to receive much direct help in terms of intelligence, air support and medical, which were key force multipliers and morale assets. ANSF appeared to grow in confidence and capability. After a few years it seemed to some like the time for tough love again: "They've come on well and can handle the insurgency on their own; let go of their hand or we'll be here for ever; they'll manage (just)." The only remaining question was when exactly, and how. US troop numbers, always the critical factor, began to reduce steadily from 2018, and in February 2020 an agreement was signed in Qatar with the Taliban which appeared to promise a peaceful exit strategy. The New York Times's bureau chief for South Asia, previously the paper's senior correspondent in Afghanistan, Mujib Mashal, wrote:

> "The agreement signed in Doha, Qatar, which followed more than a year of stop-and-start negotiations and conspicuously excluded the American-backed Afghanistan government, is not a final peace deal, is filled with ambiguity, and could still unravel.
>
> But it is seen as a step toward negotiating a more sweeping agreement that some hope could eventually end the insurgency of the Taliban, the militant movement that once ruled Afghanistan under a severe Islamic code.
>
> The war cost $2 trillion and took the lives of more than 3,500 American and coalition troops and tens of thousands of Afghans since the US invasion in aftermath of the Sept. 11 attacks, which were plotted by Al Qaeda leaders under the protection of the Taliban.
>
> The withdrawal of American troops — about 12,000 are still in Afghanistan — is dependent on the Taliban's fulfilment of major commitments that have been obstacles for years, including its severance of ties with international terrorist groups such as Al Qaeda.
>
> The agreement also hinges on more difficult negotiations to come between the Taliban and the Afghan government over the country's future. Officials hope those talks will produce a power-sharing arrangement and lasting cease-fire, but both ideas have been anathema to the Taliban in the past.
>
> 'I really believe the Taliban wants to do something to show that we're not all wasting time,' President Trump said in Washington

hours after the agreement had been signed. 'If bad things happen, we'll go back.'"

In November 2020, despite the wishes of the US joint chiefs of staff, President Trump announced further cuts (to a maximum of 2,500 in January 2021), with an aspiration for total withdrawal by 1 May 2021. In April 2021, President Biden announced that there would be total withdrawal by the highly symbolic date of 11 September – "9/11". As it would be nigh impossible to maintain the mission in the absence of the United States, all the other NATO nations announced the departure of their own troops too – a further 7,000. The UK's political and military leaders strongly opposed the US withdrawal. General Richards declared it "a sorry moment for Western grand strategy."

On 8 July 2021, the MoD announced, "As Operation Toral, the UK's contribution to NATO Resolute Support, draws to a close, a small number of UK military personnel will temporarily remain to support the transition to a new phase of UK Government support to Afghanistan… In line with the orderly and coordinated withdrawal of Nato forces which began on 1 May, the Prime Minister confirmed earlier today that the UK has now withdrawn the majority of our personnel from the country."

The Secretary of State for Defence, Ben Wallace, a former Scots Guards officer, added: "Operation Toral is drawing to an end, but our enduring support for the Afghan Security Forces and Afghan Government has not. We owe a huge debt of gratitude to all those who have served in Afghanistan over the past 20 years, particularly those who lost their lives. Their efforts have helped prevent international terrorism and set the country on the path to peace. We hope the deal struck last year will form the basis for progress. We will now continue this important work as we transition to a new phase in Afghanistan."

The "deal" quickly proved meaningless, as did Afghan capability. In the face of a well-planned and well-executed Taliban offensive, ANSF resistance crumbled, and with it the "new phase of assistance" to the Afghan government, who fled.

In August, British troops were redeployed to evacuate British nationals and former British staff eligible for relocation under the Afghan Relocation and Assistance Policy: Operation Pitting – again, a code name randomly generated, but meaning "setting someone or something in conflict or competition with"; and again strangely apt.

Troops from 16 Air Assault Brigade arrived in Kabul on 13 August to provide force protection and logistical support, with the Royal Air Force providing aircraft where necessary, along with the parallel US operation. Operation Pitting ended on 28 August after a multi-national effort that managed to evacuate over 122,000 people.

* * *

During the Afghan intervention, which began in 2001, 457 members of the United Kingdom's armed forces lost their lives, and many more sustained life-changing injuries. A good measure of that blood was shed by Light Dragoons and those under command of the regiment. Undoubtedly ISAF operations helped deny al-Qaeda a safe space from which to plan and launch attacks on the UK and its allies: no international terrorist attack was mounted from Afghanistan during those 20 years.

While Operations Herrick and Toral ultimately failed in building an Afghan army and police force that could defeat the Taliban, or even hold them in check, the British government has said that it will continue to use diplomatic and humanitarian "levers" to support Afghanistan's development and stability. It remains to be seen, however, if the attempts at development and nation-building in Afghanistan have taken deep enough root to survive and eventually outgrow the Taliban administration. On 6 March 2023, a joint statement was issued by the special envoys and representatives for Afghanistan from the EU, the UK and eight other countries, who had met the previous month to assess the situation. It began:

> The special envoys and representatives for Afghanistan:
>
> 1. Noted with grave concern the increased threat to security and stability in Afghanistan and the deterioration of the humanitarian and economic situation, with more than 28 million Afghans now in need of humanitarian aid, of whom more than half are women and children, and 6 million just 1 step from famine.
> 2. Emphasised their concern about increasing deterioration and multiple violations of human rights and fundamental freedoms of Afghans by the Taliban since August 2021, especially those of women and girls as well as members of ethnic and religious minorities and other marginalised groups.
>
> …
>
> 4. Expressed grave concern about the increasing threat of terrorist groups in Afghanistan, including ISKP, Al Qaeda, Tehrik-i-Taliban-Pakistan and others, which deeply affects security and stability inside the country, in the region and beyond, and called on the Taliban to uphold Afghanistan's obligation to deny these groups safe haven.

A second meeting, in October, reiterated its disquiet, acknowledging the "Taliban actions to tackle terrorist threats from ISIS-K[1] but express[ing] concern that some terrorist groups still reside safely inside Afghanistan and are able to plan and carry out cross-border terrorist strikes." A third meeting, in Qatar in February 2024, failed to make any discernible

1. Islamic State – Khorasan Province, a regional branch of the so-called (if misnamed) Islamic State group active in South-Central Asia, primarily Afghanistan.

progress, especially when at the last minute members of the Taliban government refused to participate.

* * *

In closing, and notwithstanding this gloomy picture, the words of John Masefield (Poet Laureate from 1930 to 1967) on the failure of the Dardanelles campaign in 1915 come to mind:

> "I began to consider the Dardanelles Campaign, not as a tragedy, nor as a mistake, but as a great human effort, which came, more than once, very near to triumph, achieved the impossible many times, and failed, in the end, as many great deeds of arms have failed, from something which had nothing to do with arms nor with the men who bore them. That the effort failed is not against it; much that is most splendid in military history failed, many great things and noble men have failed."

One thing is certain: that the effort in Afghanistan failed is not against the troops who made it.

The Light Dragoons never faltered.

Appendix I

Order of Battle for Successive Helmand Task Forces

OPERATION HERRICK 5

October 2006–April 2007:

- Deputy Commander, Combined Force Command, Afghanistan: Major-General Christopher Wilson (October 2006 to December 2006)
- Commander, International Security Assistance Force: General Sir David Richards (December 2006 to April 2007)
- HQ, 3 Commando Brigade, Brigadier Jerry Thomas RM

ANA & ANP Mentoring

- 45 Commando, Royal Marines
  - Whiskey Company
  - Zulu Company

Logistics HQ

- Commando Logistic Regiment

Other units

- The Light Dragoons
  - C Squadron
- 42 Commando, Royal Marines
  - Juliet Company
  - Kilo Company
  - Mike Company
    - 10 Troop
    - 11 Troop
  - Reconnaissance Troop
- 32nd Regiment Royal Artillery
  - 42 (Alem Hamza) Battery UAVs
- 29th Commando Regiment Royal Artillery
  - 7 (Sphinx) Battery Royal Artillery
  - 148 Commando Forward Observation Battery Royal Artillery
- 28 Engineer Regiment RE
- 59 Independent Commando Squadron, Royal Engineers

- Elements of 33 Engineer Regiment RE
- Elements of 11 Explosive Ordnance Disposal Regiment RLC
- 27 Transport Regiment RLC
- 29 Regiment RLC
- 2nd Medical Brigade, Royal Army Medical Corps
  - 22 Field Hospital
- 3 Regiment RMP
  - 174 Provost Company
- Elements of The 2nd Battalion Royal Regiment of Fusiliers (Theatre Reserve Battalion)
- The Rifle Volunteers/6 Rifles (TA)
  - Peninsula Company

OPERATION HERRICK 6

April 2007–October 2007:
- Commander, International Security Assistance Force: General Sir David Richards (April 2007 to October 2007)
- HQ, 12 Mechanised Brigade, Brigadier John Lorimer

Principal Manoeuvre Unit
- 1st Battalion, The Worcestershire and Sherwood Foresters Regiment (29th/45th Foot)*
  - B Company
  - C Company
  - D (Fire Support) Company

ANA & ANP Mentoring
- 1st Battalion, Grenadier Guards
  - Inkerman Company
  - The Queen's Company

Other units
- 12 Mechanized Brigade Reconnaissance Force (12 BRF)
  - 1 Platoon
  - 2 Platoon
  - B Troop 4/73 (Sphinx) Special Observation Post Battery RA (Detached)
- The Light Dragoons
- 2nd Royal Tank Regiment
  - Falcon Squadron
- 1st Battalion, The Royal Anglian Regiment - first unit in Afghanistan to the use the new "Vector" protected patrol vehicle
  - A (Norfolk) Company
  - B (Suffolk) Company

  - No 3 (Fighting) Company 1st Battalion The Grenadier Guards. Company was raised specifically for Herrick 6 and came under command of 1st Battalion The Royal Anglian Regiment. Company was disbanded once more on return to UK.
    - 7 Platoon
- Elements of 16th Regiment Royal Artillery
- 19th Regiment Royal Artillery
  - 5 (Gibraltar 1779–1783) Battery
- 32nd Regiment Royal Artillery
  - 57 (Bhurtpore) Battery Royal Artillery UAVs
- 39th Regiment Royal Artillery
  - Unknown Troop of MLRS
- 26 Engineer Regiment RE
- Elements of 33 Engineer Regiment RE
- Elements of 11 Explosive Ordnance Disposal Regiment RLC
- 4 Logistic Support Regiment RLC
  - 871 Postal & Courier Squadron RLC
  - Elements of 152 (Ulster) Transport Regt RLC
- 4 General Support Medical Regiment
- 2nd Medical Brigade, Royal Army Medical Corps
  - 212 Field Hospital
- Somme Company, composed mainly of elements of The London Regiment, also a platoon of Grenadier Guards and individual members of the Reserve Forces.
- 23 Pioneer Regiment RLC (187 Squadron, 519 Squadron and 206 Squadron)

In February 2007, it was announced that an additional 1,400 troops would be deployed to Afghanistan, primarily formed as a battlegroup around a light infantry battalion, the 1st Battalion The Royal Welsh (Royal Welch Fusiliers).

* Renamed as 2nd Battalion, The Mercian Regiment (Worcesters and Foresters) 01/09/07

OPERATION HERRICK 10

May 2009 –October 2009:
- Deputy Commander, International Security Assistance Force: Major-General James Dutton (May 2009 to October 2009)
- HQ 19 Light Brigade, Brigadier Tim Radford

Principal Manoeuvre Units
- 2nd Royal Tank Regiment
  - Egypt Squadron
- The Light Dragoons
- 1st Battalion, Welsh Guards

  - The Prince of Wales's Company
  - No. 2 Company
- 2nd Battalion, The Royal Welsh (Royal Regiment of Wales)
  - A Company
- The Black Watch, 3rd Battalion The Royal Regiment of Scotland – Brigade Reconnaissance Force
- 2nd Battalion, The Rifles
- 4th Battalion, The Rifles
  - B Company
  - R Company
- 2nd Battalion, The Royal Regiment of Fusiliers

ANA Mentoring
- 2nd Battalion, Mercian Regiment (Worcesters and Foresters)
  - B Company

ANP Mentoring
- Police Operational Mentoring and Liaison Team (POMLT)
- 2nd Battalion, Royal Gurkha Rifles
  - F Company

Other units
- 5th Regiment Royal Artillery
  - Unknown Battery (STA)
- 40th Regiment Royal Artillery
- 32nd Regiment Royal Artillery
- 39th Regiment Royal Artillery
  - Unknown Troop of M270 Multiple Launch Rocket System
- Elements of 33 Engineer Regiment RE
- 38 Engineer Regiment RE
- Elements of 170 (Infrastructure Support) Engineer Group, Royal Engineers
- Theatre Logistics Group - 4 Logistic Support Regiment
- Elements of 11 Explosive Ordnance Disposal Regiment RLC
- 17 Port and Maritime Regiment RLC, Royal Logistic Corps (Kabul)
- 27 Regiment RLC
  - 91 Supply Squadron
- 19 Combat Service Support Battalion, Royal Electrical and Mechanical Engineers (REME)
- 4th Battalion REME,
- 2nd Medical Regiment
- 4th Battalion, The Mercian Regiment
  - Normandy Company
- Elements of 5th Battalion Royal Regiment of Fusiliers (Kabul)
- 173rd Provost Company Royal Military Police

OPERATION HERRICK 16

May 2012–October 2012:

- Deputy Commander, International Security Assistance Force: Major-General Adrian Bradshaw (May 2012 to September 2012)
- Deputy Commander, International Security Assistance Force: Major-General Nick Carter (September 2012 to October 2012)
- HQ 12 Mechanised Brigade, Brigadier Doug Chalmers

Principal Manoeuvre Units

- The King's Royal Hussars
  - B Squadron
- 1st Battalion, Grenadier Guards
- 3rd Battalion, The Yorkshire Regiment (14th/15th, 19th and 33rd/76th Foot) (Duke of Wellington's)
  - Prince Wales's Company of 1st Battalion, Welsh Guards (Working as the operations company attached to the 3rd Battalion The Yorkshire Regiment)
- 1st Battalion, The Royal Anglian Regiment
  - A (Norfolk) Company
  - B (Suffolk) Company
  - C (Essex) Company
- Brigade Operations Company (BOC)
  - No. 3 Company, 1st Battalion Welsh Guards

ANA Mentoring

3rd Battalion, The Rifles

ANP Mentoring

- PMAG
  - 1st Battalion, Welsh Guards
    - No. 2 Company
    - Support Company
    - LD Sqn
    - QOGLR Sqn
  - 174 Provost Company, Royal Military Police
  - 7 (Royal Air Force Police) Squadron

BRF

- B Squadron The Light Dragoons and soldiers from Welsh Guards, RLC and American EOD

Other units

- The Light Dragoons
  - A Squadron

- 4 Close Support Battalion, Royal Electrical and Mechanical Engineers
- 1st Royal Tank Regiment
- 19th Regiment Royal Artillery
- Elements of 5th Regiment Royal Artillery
    - P Battery (The Dragon Troop) Royal Artillery (STA)
- 32nd Regiment Royal Artillery
    - Desert Hawk III UAV
    - Honeywell T-Hawk MAV
    - Watchkeeper UAV
- 26 Engineer Regiment RE
- 33 Engineer Regiment (EOD) RE
- 4 Logistic Support Regiment RLC
- 24 Postal, Courier & Movements Regiment RLC
- 4 Medical Regiment, Royal Army Medical Corps
- 228 Signals Squadron

Appendix II

Light Dragoons Staff Lists

The following regimental lists – orbats ("order of battle") – record the service of those at regimental duty with The Light Dragoons during the four tours in Helmand. Some who are listed did not deploy to Afghanistan during a particular tour, but in a small regiment all play a part in one way or another – training assistance, maintenance of equipment and other "rear support operations" as they are properly called.

Regimental Gazette 2007

Colonel of the Regiment: Lt Gen Sir R A Cordy-Simpson KBE CB DL

Regimental Headquarters

Commanding Officer	Lt Col H A Watson MBE
Second in Command	Maj D E Hughes RHG/D
Adjutant	Capt O G H King
Regimental CMO	Capt A Bartholomew
Operations Officer	Capt T J Dalby-Welsh
Intelligence Officer	Capt R H Villiers
Regimental Signals Officer	Capt P D Gummer
Regimental Sergeant Major	WO1 S D Folan

A Squadron

Squadron Leader	Maj E J R Kennedy
Squadron Second in Command	Capt C J Harcus
Squadron Sergeant Major	WO2 R C Cooperwaite

SHQ Troop

2Lt D Ansell
2Lt M Blakiston
2Lt J Arkell
The Hon E Lowther

Admin Troop

SSgt P S Harland
Tpr J M Hume
SSgt G Ball
Tpr L R Jones
Tpr D G Jury

B Squadron

Squadron Leader Maj J Godfrey
Squadron Second in Command Capt K J Atkinson
Squadron Sergeant Major WO2 D Bettney

SHQ Troop
Capt M Reed
Sgt D Buchan
Sgt J R W Bradley
Cpl M S Edwards
Cpl C J Brown
LCpl M C Foley
LCpl C Barnes
LCpl D J Goulding
Tpr M A Bird
Tpr S Grimston
Tpr S P Moralee

1st Troop
2Lt A C E Selby-Bennett
Sgt A McDonald
Cpl M Souter
Cpl C J Williams
LCpl C A Hatton
LCpl M A Pearce
Tpr M J Allaway
Tpr P M Harbord
Tpr B Holmes
Tpr G I Thomson
Tpr A M Walker

2nd Troop
2Lt C A Rotherham
Sgt M Braithwaite
Cpl K M Bell
Cpl D Gray
LCpl L H Iddon
LCpl M Mulkerrin
Tpr S Bailey
Tpr T J Durkin
Tpr G Evans
Tpr G McBeth
Tpr G A Taylor
Tpr L V Young

3rd Troop
2Lt M Hanbury-Tenison
Sgt S W Mahon
Cpl L J Binns
Cpl A D Knox
LCpl A Wallis
Tpr R J Attwater
Tpr L Dobbs
Tpr M Garbutt
Tpr S Maguire
Tpr A L Robson
Tpr J P N Tynan
Tpr A Wallis
Tpr A J Watson

GW Troop
2Lt J M Kayll
SSgt B Howard
Sgt C L Homewood
Cpl K E Burn
Cpl N Palmer
LCpl B R Mallinson
LCpl P F Martin
LCpl R A Yeats
Tpr L W Ankers
Tpr L D Hattswell
Tpr R J Macaskill

SP Troop
Lt R J Rugge-Price
Sgt M A Dobbs
Cpl S J Bawden
Cpl J S Lawson
LCpl C Dyke
LCpl A L Giles
Tpr K M Bensley
Tpr C W Cribbin
Tpr S A Crossman
Tpr S M Hunham
Tpr A B Mace
Tpr B Rigg
Tpr H J Trevor

Admin Troop
SSgt C Chandler
LCpl L T Murray
LCpl R Dearey
Tpr J L Mole
Tpr C Porteous
Tpr D C Wright
Tpr C J Yard

C Squadron

Squadron Leader Maj B J Warrack
Squadron Second in Command Capt W M Jelf
Squadron Sergeant Major WO2 H D Berry

SHQ Troop
Capt N M Durrans
Sgt K D Dixon
Sgt G Littlewood
Sgt D P Stansfield
Cpl M Newell
Cpl S R Sodeau
LCpl M A Boyeson
LCpl C Green
LCpl N D Moffett
LCpl N S Robertson
Tpr J Armstrong
Tpr R G Baselala
Tpr L R Bloom
Tpr N A Little

1st Troop
Lt J M Harris
Sgt A P Nolan
Cpl S A Sampher
Cpl R T A Spence
LCpl D N Leen
LCpl T C Nicollini
Tpr D S Freer
Tpr P C Lawrence
Tpr N A Little
Tpr S R Mallen
Tpr A R Owen
Tpr C D Rock
Tpr D A Wilson

2nd Troop
Lt J D Townsend-Rose
Sgt A C Thirlaway
Cpl B Buchan
Cpl S Cox
LCpl M A Bowman
Tpr J R Cooperwaite
Tpr E L T Lagilagi
Tpr R J Lowe
Tpr K McMeiken
Tpr J N Short
Tpr J T Spurgeon
Tpr R S Windmill

3rd Troop
Lt T W L Badham
Sgt M Wilkinson
Cpl M A Dawkins
Cpl S Pollock
LCpl M Costello
Tpr R J Ball
Tpr D Cameron
Tpr M Kay
Tpr R S Lynch
Tpr N E Parr
Tpr J Stamp
Tpr S A Taylor

4th Troop
SSgt N Winter
Sgt M J Lambie
Cpl L P Davidson
Cpl G P Johnson
Cpl B J Taafe
LCpl M C How
LCpl M A Robson
Tpr B L Anderson
Tpr A L Bowden
Tpr A P Cheshire
Tpr D L Dennis
Tpr A J Prior

Sp Troop
Capt S J Schofield
Sgt L Simpson
Cpl C G M Young

Admin Troop
SSgt B M Wilson
Cpl C S Badrock
Cpl S R Cooper
Cpl B R D Rix
LCpl M D Allen
LCpl M D Evans
LCpl P D Norris
LCpl K G Wilson
Tpr G M Beardshaw
Tpr L W Lomax
Tpr I Waterfield

D Squadron

Squadron Leader Maj T R Robb
Squadron Second in Command Capt A J Smith
Squadron Sergeant Major WO2 B Baston

SHQ Troop
Capt N C Claydon Swales
SSgt D Rae
Sgt S E Justice
Cpl G Mudd
LCpl A J Hirst

SL Troop
Capt S A Foster
Sgt L D Williams

TACP
Capt N W D Binnington
2Lt M R C Fyjis-Walker
Cpl P D Grahame
Cpl P Alderson
Cpl S Dine
Cpl G L Cuthbertson

Surv Tp - BRF
Cpl J L Fulcher
LCpl C M Curtis
LCpl P S Hurley
Tpr C Barnes
Tpr A G Noble
Tpr S Openshaw
Tpr R T Sproat
Tpr M L Zunze

HQ Squadron

Squadron Leader Maj S W Summerscales
Squadron Sergeant Major WO2 N K J Scott

SHQ
Cpl A Carr
Tpr D J Goulding
Tpr O L P Gray

Admin Troop
SSgt D P Lewis
Cpl J A Bettney
LCpl S Denton
Tpr D A Cameron

Comd Troop
WO2 (RSWO) A V Ruddock
SSgt S C Stott
Sgt G Armstrong
Cpl R Allford
Cpl S P Broughton
Cpl M Ford
LCpl D Marshall
LCpl J C Needham
LCpl J Stamp
LCpl J S Taylor
Tpr L Harrison
Tpr A Lillico
Tpr M P Williams

RAO (AGC (SPS))
Capt G Millen
Capt R S Edwards

WO2 (SQMS) S J Worth
SSgt D Gilmovitch
Sgt F Anderson
Sgt J M Hitchen
Sgt M A Wharton
Cpl L R Bennett
Cpl S W Hoon
Cpl J Perry
Cpl C L Smith
LCpl S Imray
LCpl K Y Knight
LCpl A D Plant
LCpl L Pretorius
Pte W R Harris
Pte P O'Malley

QM Dept
Capt G Milson
WO2 (RQMS) G Bartholomew
Sgt L M Johnson
Cpl P W Coupland
Cpl B W Haddock
LCpl M A McGuffie
LCpl K D Turner

QM(T) Dept
Capt S Jordan
WO2 (RQMS) K J Murray

SSgt T Bell
SSgt T J Brown
Sgt S Moxon
Cpl S R Cooper
Cpl S L Archer
Cpl I Dixon
LCpl M A Boylen
LCpl A J R Duncan
Tpr D R Bain
Tpr D C Wright

MT Troop
WO2 D J Robson
Sgt P T Holmes
Cpl B Pattinson
LCpl D P Clegg
LCpl C P McHale
LCpl S A Redmond
LCpl R M Stott
Tpr M Grainger
Tpr L D Holbrook
Tpr J L Mole
Tpr R M Sayer
Tpr C J Yard

Training Wing
Capt N Mustard
WO2 J M Henry
SSgt T Mustard
SSgt J R Milliband

Sgt M Bell
Sgt A G Carr
Cpl J S Anderson
Cpl K A Strong
Cpl P V Whitty
Cpl J G W Thompson

Catering (RLC)
WO2 A G Hill
Sgt S J Finch
Sgt D B Fox
Cpl V Blake
Cpl J Lacey
Cpl A P Meacham
Cpl J J Oliver
LCpl C S Badrock
LCpl A M Hunt
LCpl J A Syme
LCpl K M Telford
Pte T Conetta
Pte P D Gurung
Pte T Jabegu
Pte K Limbu
Pte S V Marston
Pte A Obeng
Pte T Rai
Pte W E Ratukove

Officers' Mess
SSgt J D Davies
Cpl C Overton

Warrant Officers' & Sergeants' Mess
Sgt B O Ducker
LCpl J J Sheard
Tpr J M Barrass

Welfare Office
Capt L A Newcombe
Sgt J F Hunter
Cpl P A Walker
Tpr R T Blakley
Pte McCann

Gymnasium
Sgt (QMSI) S P Green APTC
Cpl A S Wilson

Ration Store
Cpl P J Philpot

Stables
LCpl G Walton

Guard Room
Sgt S Deakin
Cpl S Crossland

LCpl D Stokoe
LCpl N J Mitchell

Padre
Rev J Clarke

LAD (REME)
Capt M B Horn
WO1 (ASM) S W McLennan
WO2 (AQMS) N J Willcoxson
WO2 (AQMS) D G Spencer
SSgt I Green
SSgt S H B Hensellek
SSgt R J Tittley
Sgt S G Creighton
Sgt A Cunningham
Sgt K A Deering
Sgt D D Ewen
Sgt S Henderson
Sgt D M Kelsall
Sgt S Lawson
Sgt I P Lee
Sgt D Logan
Sgt R M Moorhouse
Sgt M P O'Connor
Sgt N Peckham
Sgt R R Smith
Cpl S J Bawden
Cpl S B Bryce
Cpl D H Charman
Cpl A D Gernon
Cpl G J Godfrey
Cpl S Hameed
Cpl G A R Hooper
Cpl D M McCaskill
Cpl A J Prideaux
Cpl B S Roberts
Cpl J M Robertson
Cpl M Robinson
Cpl L M Robinson
Cpl D N Taylor
Cpl S Tshuma
LCpl J K Ford
LCpl V Gadsby
LCpl L A Howlett
LCpl A D Jacklin
LCpl D Jackson
LCpl L C Johnston
LCpl T Masiwini
LCpl M E McNeill
LCpl J W Nelson
Cfn K R Aldridge
Cfn A R Bell
Cfn D Bell
Cfn J R Cartwright
Cfn C M Curtis
Cfn A E Forster
Cfn L Hopkins
Cfn R A Johnson
Cfn A J Longburn
Cfn D P Treadgold

Regimental Gazette 2008

Colonel of the Regiment: Lt Gen Sir R A Cordy-Simpson KBE CB DL

Regimental Headquarters

Commanding Officer	Lt Col H A Watson MBE
Second in Command	Maj O J F Nurton
Adjutant	Capt T R M Robinson
RCM Officer	Capt L A Newcombe
Operations Officer	Capt S A Foster
Intelligence Officer	Capt T W L Badham
Regimental Signals Officer	Capt R J Rugge-Price
Regimental Sergeant Major	WO1 S D Folan

A Squadron

Squadron Leader	Maj A C B Pearce
Squadron Second in Command	Capt C A Rotheram
Squadron Sergeant Major	WO2 C Chandler

SHQ Troop
Sgt M Braithwaite
Cpl N D Perry
LCpl K A Lambie
LCpl M Mulkerrin
LCpl R A Yeats
Tpr D Allen
Tpr M Garbutt
Cpl M A Dawkins
LCpl C W Cribbin
Tpr P M Collins
Tpr D V P Holmes
Tpr A B Mace
Tpr H J Trevor
Tpr A D Wiles
Tpr R S Windmill

1st Troop
Lt J W M Blakiston
Sgt D Gray
Cpl B R D W J Rix
LCpl P S Hurley
LCpl R T Sproat
LCpl M L Zunze
Tpr M R Allott
Tpr L W Ankers
Tpr R G Baselala
Tpr C P Cooke
Tpr P M Harboard
Tpr D J Higgins
Tpr P E Tidmus

2nd Troop
Lt D R Ansell
Sgt P D Grahame

3rd Troop
LT E J Quicke
Sgt G Mudd
Cpl M Newell
LCpl S M Hunnam
Tpr M J Allaway
Tpr S Grimston
Tpr G A Taylor

SP Troop
Sgt C L Homewood
Cpl M A Wardle
Tpr R J Ball
Tpr A P Cheshire
Tpr M G Clayton
Tpr R J Sime
Tpr R Stanier

Admin Troop
SSgt P S Harland
Cpl P W Coupland
LCpl M D Allen
Tpr W J Thompson

B Squadron

Squadron Leader	Maj J Godfrey
Squadron Second in Command	Capt A C E Selby-Bennett
Squadron Sergeant Major	WO2 D Bettney

SHQ Troop
Sgt G Armstrong
Sgt S W Mahon
Sgt A McDonald
Cpl S W Hoon
LCpl A D Plant
LCpl M C Woods
Tpr K M Bensley
Tpr S A Crossman
Tpr G Evans
Tpr G I Thomson

1st Troop
Lt J C B Black
Sgt S Pollock
Cpl M Souter
LCpl C Barnes
Tpr D Bartholemew
Tpr R Brown
Tpr M K Cooke
Tpr L J Hunter
Tpr M G Littlewood
Tpr S P Moralee
Tpr A L Robson

2nd Troop
Lt E J Lowther
Sgt T B Dove
Cpl C J Brown
LCpl L H Iddon
LCpl J Stamp
Tpr R J Attwater
Tpr D D Beckley
Tpr L Dobbs
Tpr S Maguire
Tpr D Melvin
Tpr R C Tonge
Tpr J P N Tynan
Tpr A J Watson

SP Troop
Lt M Hanbury-Tennison
Sgt J S Lawson
Cpl R Allford
Cpl P F Martin
LCpl M Costello
LCpl A J Hirst
LCpl B R Mallinson
LCpl K D Turner
Tpr C Barrass
Tpr I K Craggs
Tpr R S Lynch
Tpr D M Macaskill
Tpr C N Timpson
Tpr L W Wilburn
Tpr J R Wright

Admin Troop
SSgt S Deakin
Cpl L J Binns
Cpl J D Nelson
Cpl E D Taylor
LCpl R Deary
Tpr P J Katimeier
Tpr J C McCartney
Tpr D C Wright

C Squadron

Squadron Leader	Maj S J Plant
Squadron Second in Command	Capt N C Claydon-Swales
Squadron Sergeant Major	WO2 D McKenzie

SHQ Troop
Sgt L D Williams
Sgt M Ford
Cpl L R Bennett
LCpl T C Abbot
LCpl R A Boyers
LCpl B R Brewer
LCpl J R Saxby
Tpr M Kay
Tpr D M McKenzie
Tpr L Wilson 621

1st Troop
Lt O E S Blake
Sgt S Crossland
Cpl R T A Spence
LCpl M A Bowman
LCpl C S Dyke
Tpr S A Ball
Tpr L R Bloom
Tpr A L Bowden
Tpr L D Hatswell
Tpr M G Longstaff
Tpr K McMeiken
Tpr M J Purvis

2nd Troop
Lt J P Arkell
Sgt K M Bell
Cpl L P Davidson
Tpr J L Coates
Tpr J R Cooperwaite
Tpr P C Lawrence
Tpr C J Lewis
Tpr L W Lomax
Tpr C D Rock
Tpr J K Smiles
Tpr D J T Tait

Sp Troop
Lt M R C Fyjis-Walker
Sgt N Lees
Sgt G Littlewood
Cpl A S Richardson
Cpl D J Bedeman
LCpl D R Bain
LCpl N D Moffett
Tpr A S Cheetham
Tpr E S Jenkins
Tpr N E Parr
Tpr A S Pembroke
Tpr O A Wilson 062

Admin Troop
SSgt N Winter
LCpl M D Evans
LCpl S R Mallen
LCpl L T Murray
LCpl J N Short
Tpr A Lillico

D Squadron

Squadron Leader	Maj R R Lyon
Squadron Second in Command	Capt N M Durrans
Squadron Sergeant Major	WO2 B M Wilson

SHQ Troop
Sgt J R W Bradley
Sgt C L Crompton
Cpl J Perry
LCpl L V Young
Tpr S M Carr
Tpr J E Dixon
Tpr S A Maule

Comd Troop
Capt R J Rugge-Price
WO2 S C Stott
SSgt M D Liddle
Sgt S Lester
Cpl A J R Duncan
Cpl S P Broughton
Cpl N S Robertson
Cpl S Cox
LCpl B J Smith
LCpl M C Foley
LCpl J S Taylor
Tpr J M Hume
Tpr M C How
Tpr N A Little
Tpr G M Beardshaw
Tpr J M Reid
Tpr J Stamp
Tpr T J Durkin
Tpr J M Barrass

SLT Troop
Capt N W D Binnington
Cpl P Alderson

TACP
Capt J M Harris
Sgt G L Cuthbertson

Surv Tp
Lt J M Kyall
SSgt B Howard
Sgt P H Bentley
Cpl K E Burn
Cpl J L Fulcher
Cpl B J Taaffe
LCpl T J Dimbleby
LCpl L D Leen
LCpl A G Noble
LCpl J T Spurgeon
Tpr S Bailey
Tpr A P Cook
Tpr D L Dennis
Tpr E L T Lagilagi
Tpr S Laurie
Tpr RJ Lowe

SQMS
SSgt D Rae
Cpl C Overton
Tpr B A Gray
Tpr S Kelly
Tpr C A Hatton

HQ Squadron

Squadron Leader Maj S P Wiles
Squadron Second in Command Capt S J Schofield
Squadron Sergeant Major WO2 N Scott

HQ
gt T Carr
gt S P Green

dmin Troop
Sgt M A Dobbs
pl P A Walker
Cpl S Denton

AO (AGC (SPS))
apt G Millen
apt S E Rowberry
O2 (SQMS) S J Worth
Sgt D Gilmovitch
gt F Anderson
gt R Burgess
gt J M Hitchen
pl L Bennett
pl S Hoon
pl J Perry
pl C Pretorius
pl C Smith
Cpl K Knight
Cpl A D Plant
Cpl P O'Malley
te W Harris-Barnett
te R Crawford

M Dept
apt A D Bartholomew
O2 (RQMS) H D Berry
t L M Johnson
Cpl L E Pattinson
Cpl B W Haddock
LCpl M A McGuffie
LCpl K M Taylor

QM(T) Dept
Capt J Jordan
WO2 (RQMS) K J Murray
SSgt T S Brown
Sgt S Moxon
Cpl S R Cooper
Cpl I Dixon
LCpl A Archer
Tpr M Grainger

MT Troop
WO2 T Bell
Sgt P Holmes
Cpl D P Clegg
Cpl R M Stott
Cpl S Dine
LCpl C McHale
Tpr S Anderson
Tpr L Holbrook
Tpr McBeth
Tpr N Widdison
Tpr C J Yard

Training Wing
Capt N Mustard
WO2 J M Henry
SSgt D Buchan
SSgt J R Milliband
Sgt J S Anderson
Sgt S J McLaren
Sgt G Mudd
Sgt L Simpson
Sgt C G M Young
Cpl S R Sodeau
Cpl K Strong
Cpl B L Thurlow
LCpl T L Mighty

Catering (RLC)
WO2 M W Williams
Sgt J J Lui
Sgt D B Fox
Cpl M Blake
Cpl J Lacey
Cpl L M Gerrie
Cpl J Oliver
LCpl A M Hunt
LCpl J Dunning
Pte T Rai
Pte B Gurung
Pte T Jabegu
Pte K Limbu
Pte S V Marston
Pte A Obeng
Pte W E Ratukove

Officer's Mess
SSgt J Davies
LCpl D Goulding

Warrant Officers' and Sergeants' Mess
Sgt B Ducker
LCpl A J Hirst
Tpr D C Colbeck

Welfare Office
Capt M Reed
Sgt J F Hunter
Tpr R T Blakley

Gymnasium
Sgt (QMSI) S Green APTC
Cpl A S Wilson

Ration Store
Cpl P J Philpot

Guard Room
Sgt M J Lambie
Cpl B Buchan
LCpl D Stokoe
LCpl Abbott
Tpr T J Cockman

Post Bunk
Cpl G Wilkinson

Padre
Rev J Clarke

LAD (REME)
Capt D J Bunker
WO1 (ASM) A McLennan
WO2 (AQMS) N J Willcoxson
SSgt D V P Baldwin
Sgt S Creighton
Sgt B S Holmes
Sgt R T Lee
Sgt D Logan
Sgt R M Moorhouse
Sgt M J Ogilvie
Sgt R R Smith
Sgt C A Church
Cpl G A Bascope
Cpl B R Haynes
Cpl L A Howlett
Cpl D M McCaskill
Cpl A J Prideaux
Cpl R Roberts
Cpl M Robinson
Cpl L M Robinson
LCpl K N Dayson
LCpl A Horridge
LCpl A Jacklin
LCpl T Masiwini
LCpl S J Shrewsbury
LCpl J R Cartwright
Cfn M R Banfield
Cfn M L Deller
Cfn A E Forster
Cfn J Hall
Cfn K Hopkins
Cfn J H Meakins
Cfn S N Peters
Cfn C M S Sheriff
Cfn T Lee

Regimental Gazette 2010

The Light Dragoons
(As at December 2009)

Colonel Of The Regiment: Maj Gen A R E de C Stewart CBE

Regimental Headquarters

Commanding Officer: Lt Col A G C Fair DSO
Second In Command: Maj H J Willis
Adjutant: Capt T R M Robinson
Assistant Adjutant: Capt S A Foster
Operations Officer: Capt J Kayll
Intelligence Officer: Capt T W L Badham
Regimental Sergeant Major: WO1 G Bartholomew
Regimental Careers Management Officer: Capt L A Newcombe
Regimental Careers Management Warrant Officer: SSgt J K Jarvis

A Squadron

Squadron Leader: Maj J Campbell-Barnard
Squadron Second In Command: Capt J C B Black
Squadron Sergeant Major: WO2 N Winter

SHQ
Sgt C J Brown
Cpl A J Cawthorne
Cpl L Lubin
Cpl A Clifton
LCpl R Windmill
LCpl G Evans
LCpl R P B Napthan
Tpr M R Allott
Tpr R J Attwater
Tpr R G Baselala
Tpr J F Gillespie
Tpr J W Learman
Tpr B A Cope
Tpr C M Morrison

1st Troop
Lt L C Doddington
Sgt M A Dawkins
Cpl C Green
LCpl A B Mace
LCpl M Souter
Tpr T L Allen
Tpr P M Collins
Tpr S Grimston
Tpr A M Hill 509
Tpr L J L Julien
Tpr G Killington-Parker
Tpr M G Clayton

2nd Troop
Lt E J Quicke
Sgt Delves
Cpl S P Dinsley
Cpl M Wardle
LCpl M K Cooke 762
LCpl D Stokoe
Tpr M Garbutt
Tpr A H Kalinte
Tpr G I Felix
Tpr M G Littlewood
Tpr D Melvin
Tpr P E Tidmus
Tpr P J Hill
Tpr N P Whale
Tpr K J Anderson
Tpr D D Beckley

3rd Troop
Lt M C Robinson
Sgt T B Dove
A/Sgt L H Iddon
Cpl P W Coupland
LCpl B R Mallinson
Tpr R J Sime
Tpr A J Deans
Tpr M Singh
Tpr L D J Head
Tpr A D Wiles
Tpr M Thurtle
Tpr R C Tonge
Tpr P Brooks 666
Tpr R A Colbeck

4th Troop
2 Lt A T B Pike
Sgt G Mudd
Sgt N P Ablett
Cpl R A Yeats
Cpl B L Thurlow
LCpl A P Cheshire
LCpl N Ryan
Tpr R Brown
Tpr G P Cooke
Tpr L J Hunter
Tpr P J Kallmeier
Tpr A L Robson
Tpr D R R Scott
Tpr B Bays
Tpr D P Riley

Admin Troop
SSgt G Armstrong
Cpl B R D W J Rix
LCpl C W Cribbin
Tpr M V Connor
Tpr P D Taylor
Tpr A J Watson
Tpr B J Stubbs

B Squadron

Squadron Leader: Maj J Chandler
Squadron Second In Command: Capt I A Carmichael
Squadron Sergeant Major: WO2 Stanfield

HQ Troop
Lt W D C Davies
Sgt Littlewood
/Sgt S Cox
Cpl M A Pearce
pl N D Perry
pl A J Hirst
pl C Williams
Cpl P O'Malley
Cpl S Coulthard
Cpl J Stamp
Cpl Colbeck 647
pr K M Bensley
pr M J Burnside
pr P J Hill
pr D L R Patterson

alaklava Troop
t M Hanbury-Tenison
VO2 A C Thirlaway
Sgt P Alderson
Sgt C L Homewood
Tpr D L Jackson
Tpr B J Moore
Tpr A Jordan
Tpr B J Kidd
Tpr K M Shepherd
Tpr R P Collyer
Tpr L A Hodson
Tpr P B Hope
Tpr T J Doble
Tpr S R Harrison
Tpr D P Jones
Tpr J W Osborne
Tpr C F Diboll
Tpr P A Duke
Tpr G W Luckman
Tpr R J Emmanuel
Tpr J A Agiadis
Tpr D Boyer
Tpr P M Calvert
Tpr S L Coles
Tpr J Moore
Tpr N Waller
Tpr C W Dunleavy
Tpr J R Ford
Tpr D S L Price
Tpr J M Williams 622
Tpr R G Gardiner
Tpr L S Wigglesworth
Tpr A D Kopicki
Tpr C A Milburn
Tpr S G Aspland
Tpr D J Roderick-Jones
Tpr G F Patterson
Tpr T J Hutchinson
Tpr J M Williams 118
Tpr S S English
Tpr S F G Cooper
Tpr D E E Laylak
Tpr M S Reynolds
Tpr K Evans
Tpr R Groenewald
Tpr D J Bisby
Tpr D L Williams 727
Tpr C Jacka
Tpr M Lloyd
Tpr N A Nutton
Tpr R Clark
Tpr O Orotoma
Tpr M J Allaway
Tpr N S Thorley
Tpr D A Knewstubb
Tpr P P Maynard
Tpr J D Purdy
Tpr C A Metcalf
Tpr J Simpson
Tpr S J Whiting
Tpr A Oldham
Tpr M I Atkinson
Tpr A R Marsh
Tpr W A Ward
Tpr S A Welsh
Tpr J A Campbell
Tpr J L Hewson
Tpr S P Fitzgerald
Tpr A R Morrell
Tpr B Holmes
Tpr J C McCartney
Tpr W Thompson
Tpr B M Swift
Tpr W S Pennington
Tpr M S Rutherford
Tpr D L McGrath
Tpr C A Farrell
Tpr J J Aviss
Tpr G A Taylor

C Squadron

Squadron Leader: Maj S Plant
Squadron Second In Command: Capt N C Claydon-Swales
Squadron Sergeant Major: WO2 M Wilkinson

HQ
gt M Ford
Cpl T C Abbot
Cpl B R Brewer
Cpl M Townley
Cpl R J Crawford
pr R Bull
pr J A Clapham
pr M S Harris
pr M Kay
pr D J Tait

t Troop
Lt H A H Amos
t S Crossland
pl C S Dyke
pl M C Woods
Cpl L R Bloom
LCpl A L Bowden
Tpr S A Ball
Tpr L J Coleman
Tpr S A Crossman
Tpr L Keen
Tpr K McMeiken
Tpr D K L Larkin

2nd Troop
Lt C W L Dunn
Sgt K M Bell
Cpl D J Bedemann
Cpl A Richardson
LCpl C D Rock
Tpr J Bradley
Tpr J Coates
Tpr S Hutchinson
Tpr C J Lewis
Tpr J K Smiles
Tpr G I Thomson

3rd Troop
Lt G F Disney
Sgt J S Lawson
Cpl M A Bowman
Cpl M Costello
LCpl A P Cook
LCpl K D Turner
Tpr J I Chapman
Tpr D M Macaskill
Tpr P L Maddren
Tpr A J A Wild
Tpr J R Wright

4th Troop
Lt T D R Gregg
Sgt N Lees
Cpl J N Short
LCpl C Goodey
LCpl J R Saxby
Tpr M D Black
Tpr M J Hardy
Tpr E S Jenkins
Tpr T W Laws
Tpr C A Orwin
Tpr M J Purvis
Tpr D S Thomson
Tpr M A Watson

5th Troop
2 Lt W E D Carver
SSgt C Loughney
Cpl S J Talyor
LCpl R E Edge
Tpr A S Cheetham
Tpr N G Guffick
Tpr A L Matthews
Tpr K D Leech
Tpr L W Willburn

Admin Troop
SSgt S Deakin
Cpl A A Evans
Cpl K G Wilson
LCpl A Lillico
LCpl L T Murray
LCpl O A Wilson
Tpr J P Armer
Tpr D H Craggs
Tpr L D Hatswell
Tpr O L Imam

D Squadron

Squadron Leader: Maj C Palmer
Squadron Second In Command: Capt J M Harris
Squadron Sergeant Major: WO2 P S Harland

Command Troop
Capt D Ansell
WO2 B P Kershaw
SSgt C L Crompton
Sgt S Lambie
Cpl S J Talyor
Cpl A J R Duncan
Cpl D N Leen
Cpl C Overton
Cpl P J Somers
LCpl G M Beardshaw
LCpl J R Cooperwaite
LCpl J M Hume
LCpl E L T Lagilagi
LCpl N A Little
LCpl R J Lowe
Tpr C Barrass
Tpr J M Barrass
Tpr R J Bix
Tpr L Dobbs
Tpr B A Gray
Tpr T W Holden
Tpr S Maguire
Tpr J M Reid
Tpr C N Reddin

TACP
Capt P A Douglas
Sgt G L Cuthbertson
Cpl R Allford
Cpl B Buchan
Cpl M C Foley
Cpl N S Robertson
LCpl T J Dimbleby
LCpl M C How

BRF
Capt E Lowther
SSgt L Simpson
LCpl S R Mallen
LCpl B J Smith
Tpr D Bartholomew
Tpr S Laurie

OMLT
Lt J P Arkell
SSgt M A Dobbs
Sgt P H Bentley
Sgt J L Fulcher
Cpl L J Binns
Cpl B W Haddock
Cpl P F Martin
LCpl Tynan
LCpl K Bensley
LCpl G Beardshaw
LCpl D Cameron

Admin Tp
SSgt B Howard
LCpl J Spurgeon
Tpr D R Bain
Tpr J E Dixon

HQ Squadron

Squadron Leader: Maj R E Wiles
Squadron Second In Command: Capt D A Smith
Squadron Sergeant Major: WO2 D Buchan

SHQ and Admin Trp
WO2 S Stott
Sgt K Turner
Sgt J Anderson
Cpl P A Walker
Tpr R Lynch
Tpr L Lomax
Pte T T R Fuller
Tpr J J Southall-Owan
Tpr G Hamilton
Tpr A Barnett
Tpr N J Weston
Tpr C H Clifton
Tpr B P Kershaw
Tpr M T Nicholson
Tpr C Wiborg
Tpr R J Clubley

LAD (REME)
Capt D Bunker
WO1 S Mclennan
WO2 N Willcoxson
SSgt G Baldwin
SSgt I Dockree
SSgt B Hall
SSgt A Murray
Sgt A Atkinson
Sgt C Church
Sgt R Denwood
Sgt G Lancaster
Sgt M Ogilvie
Sgt N Peckham
Sgt S Ross
Sgt D Ramsay
Sgt A Venner
Sgt D Wright
Cpl G Bascope
Cpl S Bawden
Cpl H Breed
Cpl K Dayson
Cpl S Deacon
Cpl A Evans
Cpl B Haynes
Cpl A Horridge
Cpl R Lord
Cpl D McLennan
Cpl A Trueman
Cpl A Wilson
Cpl S Peters
LCpl K Aldridge
LCpl M Banfield
LCpl J Cartwright
LCpl D Clarke
LCpl D Crick
LCpl K Crockford
LCpl J Gould
LCpl D Grey
LCpl J Henderson
LCpl D Jackson
LCpl S Mellor
LCpl A Slane
Cfn V Dube
Cfn T Lee
Cfn J Meakins
Cfn D Miller
Cfn D Palmer
Cfn C Sheriff

AGC Det
Capt H Sparks
Lt B D Buckenham
WO2 S Williams
SSgt D Cade
Sgt K May
Sgt G A Gittins
Sgt J Whitehouse
Cpl Reade
Cpl Grundy
Cpl Drew
LCpl R A J Veikoso
Pte M S O Devine
Pte P Singh

Post Bunk
Cpl G Wilkinson

Welfare Office
Capt M Reed
Sgt M Braithwaite

Gymnasium
Sgt (QMSI) S Green
LCpl J P N Tynan

QM Dept
Maj A D Bartholomew
WO2 (RQMS) D Rae
Sgt L E Johnson
Cpl M Boyeson
Cpl M A McGuffie
Cpl I Dixon
LCpl K J Taylor

Officers' Mess
SSgt S Mahon
LCpl D J Goulding
LCpl P S Hurley
Tpr S Bailey

Warrant Officers' and Sergeants' Mess
Sgt L Backhouse
Tpr J E Dixon

QM(T) Dept
Capt K J Murray
WO2 (RQMS)
J D Davies
Sgt S Moxon
gt S Cooper
Cpl A Archer
Cpl S Denton
LCpl M Allen
Tpr S Kelly
Tpr N Parr

Catering (RLC)
WO2 M W Williams
gt G Baker
Sgt A Faben
Cpl L M Gerrie
Cpl J Lacey
Cpl J Oliver
Cpl N Walker
LCpl J Dunning
LCpl A M Hunt
LCpl T Rai
LCpl K B Zaayman
Pte D Johnson
Pte T Jabegu
Pte K Limbu
Pte S V Marston
Pte Nedin
Pte L P Rai
Pte W E Ratukove
Pte A Yakubu
Pte M S N Sangiang

Ration Store
LCpl T Conetta

MT Troop
Capt D A Smith
WO2 T Bell
Sgt B Ducker
Sgt P Holmes
Cpl D Clegg
Cpl C McHale
Cpl R M Stott
LCpl C Yard
Tpr L W Ankers
Tpr R G Basealala
Tpr J Brooks 993
Tpr M V Connor
Tpr I Costello
Tpr J Garsrud
Tpr J Kelsey
Tpr S King
Tpr H Trevor
Tpr D C Wright

Training Wing
Capt S D Folan
WO2 ME Ramsden
SSgt M Bell
Sgt Macleod
Sgt Turner
Sgt K E Burn
Sgt Whear
Sgt S Pettit
Cpl R E W Hindson
LCpl Napthen

Guard Room
Sgt S Polluck
LCpl L V Young
LCpl M Williams
Tpr M Brown

Regimental Gazette 2013

The Light Dragoons
(As at September 2012)

Colonel of the Regiment	Maj Gen A R E de C Stewart CB CBE

Regimental Headquarters

Commanding Officer	Lt Col S J Plant MBE
Second in Command	Maj J M Godfrey
Adjutant	Capt The Hon. E J Lowther
Operations Officer	Capt N C Claydon-Swales
Regimental Careers Management Officer	Capt A V Ruddock
Intelligence Officer	Lt A L R Werner Int Corps
Regimental Sergeant Major	WO1 D Rae

A Squadron

Squadron Leader	Maj W R G Leek SCOTS DG
Second in Command	Capt L C Doddington
Squadron Sergeant Major	WO2 B Howard

SHQ
Capt W M C Tod
Sgt K D Dixon
Sgt M Shaw RE
Cpl J S Taylor
Cpl M Souter
Cpl R P B Napthan RAMC
LCpl S Maguire
LCpl L R S Robson RAMC
LCpl J R Wright
Tpr P M Brooks
Tpr J C McCartney
Tpr P J Hill
Tpr M V Connor
Tpr T Coleman
Tpr A J Watson
Tpr S C Pickard
Tpr L J L Julien
Tpr J Simpson
Tpr J W Osborne
Tpr J R Marshall

1st Troop
Lt W J McManners
Sgt M Newell
Cpl A J Cawthorne
LCpl A L Russell
LCpl J R Cooperwaite

2nd Troop (Det PAT)
Lt J Harle
Sgt M A Bowman
Cpl S R Mallen
LCpl T C Abbott
LCpl K O M Evans
Tpr A R Marsh
Tpr C J Middleton
Tpr J W Learman
Tpr A D Johnston
Tpr A Jordan
Tpr J R Jeavons
Tpr T R Hewitt
Tpr J M Taylor
Tpr J M Egan

3rd Troop
Lt R P Glover
Sgt S A Sampher
Cpl N Ryan
Cpl A L Bowden
LCpl R J Sime
LCpl N J Weston
Tpr N A Nutton
Tpr M G Purvis
Tpr D A Hodgson
Tpr R Clark
Tpr A N Owen
Tpr J M Gargan
Tpr W S Pennington

4th Troop (Det PAT)
Lt E C Whitten
Sgt L P Davidson
Cpl M D Evans
LCpl D L Hunter
LCpl A W Fernandez
LCpl M C Thurtle
LCpl L Wilson
Tpr J D Purdy
Tpr S J Harrison
Tpr S S English
Tpr G R Wilson
Tpr L Jenney
Tpr M I Atkinson

5th Troop (Det PAT)
Lt R G S Luckyn-Malone
Sgt L H Iddon
Cpl T E Harper
Cpl L R Bloom
LCpl L T Keen
Tpr M A Watson
Tpr T J Hutchinson
Tpr L N Brook
Tpr G W Luckman
Tpr D S L Price
Tpr J A Agiadis
Tpr G I Felix

SQMS Troop
SSgt S Crossland
Cpl M A Boyeson
Cpl P F Martin
Cpl C Barnes
LCpl N Widdison
LCpl S Grimston
LCpl T W Pearce
LCpl O Orotoma
Tpr S A Chalkley

LAD
SSgt A J Wigg
Sgt S McConville
Cpl R K Prettyman
Cpl I H Hayes
Cpl C J Newton
LCpl M G W Blow
LCpl H A Hussain
Cfn G M Williams
Cfn M S Topping
Cfn M A Tidmus
Cfn A E Hunt

B Squadron

Squadron Leader	Maj T J Dalby-Welsh
Second in Command	Capt C S N Fenton WG
Squadron Sergeant Major	WO2 C J Loughney

HQ
VO2 T B Dove
gt J Stamp
pl A Pallatina QARANC
Cpl N J Aspinall RAMC
Cpl S J Dalby
Cpl L D J Head
te D-L Hewitson AGC

QMS
Sgt G P Johnson
gt A Hernandez REME
pl K G Wilson

1st Troop
Capt H A H Amos
Lt I R Massey
CSgt J E Geen WG
Sgt J N Short
Sgt B J Taaffe
Cpl I W Jackson RAMC
Cpl M L Caswell REME
Cpl J Cooke
LCpl L D Hatswell
LCpl M G Littlewood
LCpl R Brown
Tpr A L Couling
Tpr B K Burdett
Tpr J Moore
Tpr M S Goodall
Tpr C S M Batty
Tpr C F Diboll
Tpr G S Roos
Tpr M N Appleby
Tpr J J Southall-Owen
Tpr A Nutton

2nd Troop
Capt W D C Davies
Lt L G Twyman
Sgt A Richardson
Cpl C S Dyke
LCpl Reddin
LCpl G I Thomson
LCpl C W Dunleavy
LCpl W A Moloney
Tpr S R Astwood
Tpr L A Hodson
Tpr L Hubbard
Tpr E M Leung
Tpr P E Burt
Tpr D G A Lawton
Tpr D A Vann
Tpr L K Peacock
Tpr D L Potts
Tpr M S Reynolds
Tpr C F Klopper
Cfn D J Lougher REME
Tpr D J Roderick-Jones
Tpr M D Skeavington
Tpr C R Richardson

3rd Troop
SSgt L Simpson
Sgt C J Williams
Cpl B R Brewer
Cpl A P Cheshire
Cpl R D Edge
LCpl C A Milburn
LCpl A S Limbu RAMC
RAMC LCpl T W Holden
Tpr J B Moss
Tpr M Sykes
Tpr P J Helliwell
Tpr L P Fox
Tpr D J Kenney
Tpr P A Duke
Tpr J J Avis
Tpr A Oldham
Tpr J L Hewson
Tpr A H Kalinte
Tpr B Rowson
Tpr B T Richards
Tpr J P Lough
Tpr D Maguire
Tpr Royce

C Squadron

Squadron Leader	Maj R D Scott
Second in Command	Capt N W D Binnington MBE
Squadron Sergeant Major	WO2 S Deakin

HQ
Sgt J S Lawson
pl D A Thomasson AGC
pl I F McMorrow RE
Cpl M S Muzavazi AGC
Cpl M Singh
pr M J Smith
pr J B Spiring
pr B M Swift
pr S O Telford
pr A Tinnion
pr K C Simmonds
pr D L Waites
pr W A Ward
pr D L Williams

2nd Troop
SSgt G Mudd
Cpl D Marshall
Cpl C W Cribben
Cpl E L T Lagilagi
LCpl M K Cooke
LCpl D Bartholomew
LCpl P O'Malley
Tpr T R Bettles
Tpr I J Carey
Tpr J Bonnefoy
Tpr P M W Newman
Tpr J A Clapham
Tpr B De Villiers
Tpr R A P Dry
Tpr L D Green
Tpr D L Hunter
Tpr M R Keen
Tpr M C Maguire
Tpr A R Milley
Tpr J M Williams
Tpr J R Oughtred
Tpr N R Reid
Tpr D J Sewell

SQMS
SSgt J L Bower
Cpl J Selman
LCpl L Dobbs
Tpr J M Bray
Tpr T Whitby
Tpr S J Whiting

LAD
Sgt I P Calton
Cpl A Bawden
LCpl D M G Clarke
LCpl M G Lidbury
LCpl L M Morris
LCpl O L J Stanton
Cfn A P Mustard
Cfn A P Allen
Cfn B T Whisker

1st Troop
SSgt M A Dawkins
Sgt S P Broughton
Cpl C Overton
Cpl A Archer
Cpl J P N Tynan
LCpl R Groenewald
LCpl D R Bain
Tpr D-L R Patterson
Tpr O J Bisby
Tpr R J Clubley
Tpr C N Bowden
Tpr A R Brittain
Tpr A Du Plessis
Tpr S R Harrison
Tpr D D Beckley
Tpr D R Liddell
Tpr S P Matthews
Tpr R J Mitchell
Tpr C A Orwin
Tpr M A Paterson
Tpr C S Rennison
Tpr A L Reeve

3rd Troop
2Lt J M H Pullinger
SSgt E D Taylor
Sgt B W Haddock

Cpl A P Cook
Cpl R G Baselala
Cpl J T Spurgeon
LCpl H K Ocadilaig
LCpl E S Jenkins
Tpr G A Killington-Parker
Tpr C G Coombs
Tpr D Boyer
Tpr W T Carney
Tpr J K Ellis
Tpr P B Hope
Tpr D W Johnson
Tpr J L Longford
Tpr A R McDonnell
Tpr L N Molics
Tpr P P Maynard
Tpr A A Pearson
Tpr L Scotting
Tpr H L Simpson

D Squadron

Squadron Leader Maj C T Colbeck
Second in Command Capt W E D Carver
Squadron Sergeant Major WO2 P M Stone

SHQ
SSgt P D Grahame
Sgt L J Moon
Cpl J R E Price
Cpl M J Purvis
LCpl A S Cheetham

TACP
Capt G F Disney
Sgt N S Robertson
Sgt S Dine
Cpl B R Mallinson
Cpl M C Foley
LCpl T R Doble
LCpl C M Morrison
LCpl K B Quartey RAMC

KRH BG
Maj S J A Ward
LCpl J Kelsey
Tpr Clayton
Tpr J Blacklock
Tpr C Brown
Tpr J I Chapman
Tpr C Hoe
Tpr C A Metcalfe
Tpr A A Ord
Tpr N S Thorley
Tpr D P Clegg
Tpr K Marsden
Tpr D R Patterson
Cfn R Stringer REME

Training Team 1
Sgt P N Morse APTC
Sgt S A Fyfe
Cpl A Lillico
Cpl M G Chard
LCpl M D Black
LCpl J K Smiles
Tpr R J Emmanuel
Tpr L S Torbitt
Tpr K D Turner
Tpr K N Wilson
Tpr D J Scammel

PMAG BG
Capt T D R Gregg MC
LCpl S A Shaw RAMC

Op BEEK (Det EOD&S)
LCpl S A Crossman
Tpr G Hamilton

Training Team 2
Sgt J W F Cairns RE
Sgt R T A Spence
Cpl J Coultard
Cpl M A Pearce
Cpl G J Delaney
LCpl M Garbutt
Tpr C W McDougal
Tpr J M Williams
Tpr A P Differ
Tpr D P Jones

Grenadier Guards BG
Lt J P Vaughan

PAT Team
Capt J F Clacy
Sgt B R D Rix
Sgt D J Bedemann
LCpl M J Burnside
LCpl R D Bunney RAMC
LCpl A J A Wild
Tpr A W H Ryde
Tpr R A P Ward
Tpr G J Tate

Royal Anglian BG
Capt H C Freeman

HQ Squadron

Squadron Leader Maj G Milson
Second in Command Capt G Bartholomew
Squadron Sergeant Major WO2 D Stanfield

Brigade Troops Echelon QM Dept
Maj S D Folan
WO2 A C Thirlaway
SSgt M Ford
Sgt M D Allen
Cpl T J Dimbleby
Cpl I Dixon
Cpl M A McGuffie
LCpl R A Yeats
LCpl D M Macaskill
LCpl S A Ball
LCpl K McMeiken
LCpl R S Windmill

(Det JFSp(A))
WO2 M Braithwaite

MT Dept
Sgt B Buchan
Cpl C P McHale
LCpl C J Yard
(Det Kabul)
LCpl P L Maddren
(Det JFSp(A))
Tpr M S Rutherford
Tpr K A Anderson
Sgt N Ncube
Cpl J T Dabire

RAO (AGC)
Lt E J Bassett
SSgt S Young
Sgt J L Whitehouse
Cpl A M Reade
Pte L M Weston
Pte M P Latham
(Det JFSp(A))
Sgt K L Robinson

LAD
Capt C J Watson
WO1 C Lye
WO2 A J Stephens
Cfn L G Stubbs
(Det 3 Rifles)
Sgt P Harrison

Catering (RLC)(Det JFSp(A)
Sgt J D Tanswell RLC
LCpl N Limbu RLC
LCpl M McDaid RLC
LCpl L P Rai RLC
Pte Sanyang RLC

Welfare (Det Engrs and EOD&S Gp)
Maj NE Allison RAChD

ISTAR Gp HQ
Capt C W L Dunn
Capt N J Taylor
Sgt R Allford
Sgt M C Woods
LCpl P M Collins
(Det TFH)
WO2 G L Cuthbertson

Rear Operations Group QM
Capt M Reed MBE
Capt D F Tims QRH
Capt M T Flitcroft FTRS
WO2 M Wilkinson
SSgt C L Homewood
Sgt S Cox
Cpl B J Smith
Cpl N A Little
Cpl S Denton
LCpl J M Hume
LCpl P E Tidmus
Tpr D P Riley
Tpr D A Knewstubb
Tpr P M Calvert
Tpr L Bajo
Tpr D K L Larkin

MT
WO2 S Lester
Sgt A Clifton
Cpl G McBeth
LCpl N E Parr
Tpr P D Branley

Provost
Cpl D J Dean
LCpl G Evans
Sgt J O John
Pte P D Singh
Pte O J Smith
Pte K-A N Taylor

RAO (AGC)
Capt P Garnett
WO2 G L Jones

LAD
SSgt I M Carpenter
Sgt R A Black
Sgt R G J Cooley
Cpl B D Curtis
Cpl M K Wiseman
LCpl J Naisbitt
LCpl J R Rivers
LCpl K D Selleck
LCpl D A Williamson
LCpl A Hill
Cfn T S Lindsey
Cfn E T Osifo Doe
Cfn D Wilson
Cfn J S Roden

RAP
Maj B M R Coghill RAMC

Trg Wng
WO2 J K Jarvis
Sgt S J Brown
Cpl D J Goulding
LCpl T R Ndlovu

Gymnasium
Cpl J B Brooke REME
LCpl D J Higgins

MPGS (AGC)
SSgt M O Field
Sgt W T Mackie
Cpl A Jackson
Cpl C Johnson
Cpl G M Burgess
LCpl B P Jackson
LCpl J W Bowie
LCpl P R Boyd
LCpl P D Savill
Pte St-J S Cooper
Pte S R Keates
Pte A Jaggs

Messes
SSgt J D Nelson
Sgt P Walker
LCpl D J W Spamer

Welfare
Capt S C Stott
SSgt J S Anderson
Sgt D Cameron
LCpl J Dunning
LCpl L V Young
Tpr A D Kopicki
Tpr M R Allott

Chefs (RLC)
Sgt A W Ineichen
Cpl N R Walker
Cpl S W Dunn

LCpl D L Haddon
LCpl J A Hutchins
Pte D A Johnson
Pte A Yakubu
Pte G Humangwa
Pte W E Ratukove
Pte G A N Wickham

Index